Deep vein thrombosis and pulmonary embolism

A guide for practitioners

Other Clinical Care books from M&K

Routine Blood Results Explained 2/e
ISBN: 978-1-905539-38-3 · 2007

The Management of COPD in Primary and Secondary Care
ISBN: 978-1-905539-28-4 · 2007

Issues in Heart Failure Nursing
ISBN: 978-1-905539-00-0 · 2006

Arterial Blood Gas Analysis: an easy learning guide
ISBN: 978-1-905539-04-8 · 2008

Primary Care Case Studies for Nurse Practitioners
ISBN: 978-1-905539-23-9 · 2008

Self-assessment in Limb X-ray Interpretation
ISBN: 978-1-905539-13-0 · 2006

Self-assessment in Paediatric Musculoskeletal Trauma X-rays
ISBN: 978-1-905539-34-5 · 2008

Paediatric Minor Emergencies
ISBN: 978-1-905539-35-2 · 2008

Eye Emergencies: the practitioner's guide
ISBN: 978-1-905539-08-6 · 2008

The Clinician's Guide to Chronic Disease Management for Long Term
Conditions: a cognitive-behavioural approach
ISBN: 978-1-905539-15-4 · 2008

Deep vein thrombosis and pulmonary embolism

A guide for practitioners

Dr Andrew Blann
PhD FRCPath

Consultant Clinical Scientist and
Honorary Senior Lecturer in Medicine

University Department of Medicine
City Hospital, Dudley Road
Birmingham B18 7QH

Deep Vein Thrombosis and Pulmonary Embolism: a guide for practitioners
Andrew Blann

ISBN: 978-1-905539-51-2

First published 2009

British Library Catalogue in Publication Data
A catalogue record for this book is available from the British Library

Notice
Clinical practice and medical knowledge constantly evolve. Standard safety precautions must be followed, but, as knowledge is broadened by research, changes in practice, treatment and drug therapy may become necessary or appropriate. Readers must check the most current product information provided by the manufacturer of each drug to be administered and verify the dosages and correct administration, as well as contraindications. It is the responsibility of the practitioner, utilising the experience and knowledge of the patient, to determine dosages and the best treatment for each individual patient. Any brands mentioned in this book are as examples only and are not endorsed by the Publisher. Neither the publisher nor the authors assume any liability for any injury and/or damage to persons or property arising from this publication.

The Publisher

To contact M&K Publishing write to:
M&K Update Ltd · The Old Bakery · St. John's Street
Keswick · Cumbria CA12 5AS

Tel: 01768 773030 · Fax: 01768 781099
publishing@mkupdate.co.uk
www.mkupdate.co.uk

Designed and typeset by Mary Blood   ·
Printed in England by Jade Print, Leeds

Contents

List of figures, tables and flowcharts

Abbreviations used in the text

ACS	Acute coronary syndrome
APTT	Activated partial thromboplastin time
BMI	Body mass index
BSH	British Society for Haematology
CABG	Coronary artery bypass graft
CCF	Congestive cardiac failure
COPD	Chronic obstructive pulmonary disease
DVT	Deep vein thrombosis
FFP	Fresh frozen plasma
GECS	Graduated elastic compression stockings
HIT	Heparin-induced thrombocytopenia
HRT	Hormone replacement therapy
IHD	Ischaemic heart disease
INR	International normalised ratio
IPC	Intermittent pneumatic compression
LMWH	Low molecular weight heparin
NPSA	National Patient Safety Agency
OCP	Oral contraceptive pill
PCI	Percutaneous coronary intervention
PE	Pulmonary embolism
TPA	Tissue plasminogen acitivator
TURP	Transurethral resection of the prostate
UFH	Unfractionated heparin
VCF	Vena cava filter
VTE	Veno-thromboembolism or veno-thromboembolic event

Introduction

Key words, when first mentioned, are formatted in **bold** *and will be explained in the Glossary.*

Venous thromboembolism

Many common problems in clinical medicine and general practice relate to arterial and venous thrombosis. Thrombosis in veins (i.e. **venous thromboembolism, [VTE]**) is a permanent problem in various cancers and following surgery, especially orthopaedic. Other risk factors include diabetes, smoking and obesity. It has recently been estimated that death due to VTE in the European Community exceeds those due to AIDS, breast cancer, prostate cancer and road traffic accidents *combined* (House of Commons Health Committee, 2005)

Pathology

A clot (thrombus) may consist simply of blood **platelets** stuck together with the glue-like **fibrin**, although red blood cells and white blood cells may also get caught up in the clot. A thrombus may form in the blood, or may develop from, and stick to, the inside of the blood vessel, from which anchored point it may grow. However, fragments (**emboli**) of this anchored clot may break off and fly away into the blood to cause problems elsewhere.

Recognition

The problem areas are clots in veins of the leg (**deep vein thrombosis: DVT**) and clots in the lungs (**pulmonary embolus: PE**) – clearly, each have their own different sets of signs and symptoms. These conditions are very well recognised and there are several aids to diagnosis, such as probability scores and laboratory tests.

Prevention and treatment

Ideally, prevention of VTE is by the avoidance (or minimisation) of risk factors such as poor diet and lack of exercise, but if this is impossible (e.g. surgery, cancer), there are drug and non-drug treatments which are also used once a clot is present.

Anti-thrombotic agents have been developed and the many classes of agents that are available are an attempt to find solutions to the wide range of thrombus-related disorders needing treatment. Without doubt the most commonly used agents in **prophylaxis** and treatment of VTE are **heparin** and **warfarin**.

Despite the widespread use of these two agents, they are rarely either totally effective or without disadvantages such as the tendency to cause bleeding, so that there is still room for drugs that act with more precision. Another group of agents, such as streptokinase, may be used in an attempt to destroy or lyse the clot once it has been formed (i.e. thrombolysis).

Aims of this book

Having worked systematically through all the material in this book, completing the *Consolidation* questions for each chapter in turn, you will:

- Appreciate the 'nuts and bolts' aspects of coagulation: how a clot forms from fibrin and platelets, and then how the body eliminates a clot once it has served its purpose.

- Recognise that the breakdown in haemostasis leads to excessive clotting in arteries and veins, the latter being venous thromboembolism (VTE).

- Identify key clinical features of the two different types of VTE:
  - deep vein thrombosis (DVT)
  - pulmonary embolus (PE).

- Be aware of additional methods for defining and assessing VTE.

- Use established and formal guidelines to consider risk stratification of DVT and PE.

- Decide on types of treatment:
  - drug treatment
  - non-drug treatment.

- Consider patient self-management according to guidelines.

- Have an awareness of the risks of, and responses to haemorrhage.

Finally, knowledge is without value if there is no practice. However, recall your limitations and work to your established clinical guidelines which should have been set and formalised by your Trust, PCT or Practice.

What are deep vein thrombosis and pulmonary embolism and why are they important?

Clots often get a bad press, but in their place they are essential in minimising blood loss (**haemorrhage**). The process of healthy clot formation, **coagulation**, is generally very tightly regulated, but when this control goes wrong it can lead to build up of clot that can then lead to clinically important thrombosis, which may even be fatal.

How coagulation works

A clot (thrombus) is formed from the **platelets** and **fibrin**. Platelets are tiny bodies produced (like red and white blood cells) in the bone marrow. The glue-like fibrin is formed from **fibrinogen**, produced by the liver. Fibrinogen gets converted into fibrin by the crucial clotting enzyme **thrombin**, a molecule so active that it cannot exist by itself in the plasma, but circulates in blood in an inactive form as **prothrombin**, which is also produced by the liver. Prothrombin is converted into thrombin by a collection of other coagulation factors (Factor VII, Factor X, calcium) and molecules that together are known as the prothrombinase complex.

Many of us will be aware of the most well-known bleeding disease, **haemophilia**. This is caused by the lack of a particular coagulation protein, **Factor VIII**. The coagulation pathway itself is generally a well regulated cascade of some 20 such coagulation factors, all acting in strict order. Fortunately, it is not important to know the full workings of this pathway in order to be a fully competent Thrombosis Practitioner. However, for completeness, Figure 1.1 (page 6) shows how these many different molecules act together to generate a fibrin clot.

The coagulation pathway cannot run indefinitely, otherwise we would all clot to death. A series of regulators keep the coagulation pathway in check. The principle inhibitors are **anti-thrombin**, **protein S** and **protein C**, all produced by the liver.

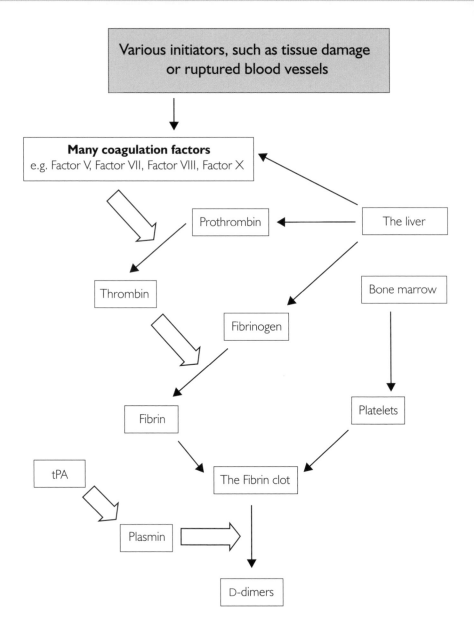

Figure 1.1 The coagulation system simplified

Small arrows indicate direct pathways in clot formation. Large open arrows indicate the action of enzyme activators of coagulation (the 'prothombinase' complex, thrombin) and of fibrinolysis (tPA, plasmin).

They become activated a few crucial seconds after the coagulation pathway itself becomes activated, and eventually catch it up and then close it down.

So once a clot has been formed, and it has done its job, it must be removed by a process called **fibrinolysis**. This is managed by the blood enzyme **plasmin**, which digests the fibrin strands. These bits of chopped-up clots in the plasma can be detected in the laboratory, and of these fragments, D-**dimers** are the most useful. Thus increased D-dimers are evidence of fibrinolysis, and so of the presence of a clot being resolved.

Coagulation is a dynamic process. The view that clotting stops and starts in a very defined way, with exact on/off signals, is now becoming obsolete. The current view suggests that we are all clotting ourselves all the time, all over the body. Fortunately, we are also dissolving these clots just as fast (by fibrinolysis) so that they do not (generally) become a problem. However, if the clot-making pathway is quicker than the clot-inhibiting and clot-breaking pathways, then thrombosis can occur.

Several factors start the coagulation 'cascade', such as crush injuries, severe bacterial infections or severed blood vessels that expose collagen. Among the first coagulation factors to be activated are **Factor V** and **Factor VII**. A major inhibitor of Factor V is Protein C.

Later, **Factor X** becomes activated and so is referred to as Factor Xa. The activity of this molecule is inhibited by Low Molecular Weight Heparin (LMWH), and Factor Xa is a major contributor to the complex of Factors and other molecules that form a so-called '**prothombinase**' complex, the function of which is to convert prothrombin into thrombin.

Once formed, thrombin acts on fibrinogen to turn it into fibrin. However, the activity of thrombin is regulated by another inhibitor, anti-thrombin. Heparin works by promoting the activity of anti-thrombin. Fibrin forms a mesh that, with platelets and other blood cells, generates a thrombus (clot) to reduce blood flow.

Fibrinolysis is the dissolution of a clot. A thrombus is digested by the enzyme plasmin, which needs to be activated by **tissue plasminogen activator** (tPA). The products of the digestion of a fibrin clot are D-dimers.

Haemostasis

Haemostasis is therefore the overall balance between coagulation (thrombus formation) and fibrinolysis (thrombus removal):

- When the balance falls in favour of coagulation, the result is thrombosis
- When the balance falls in favour of fibrinolysis, the result is haemorrhage.

Venous thrombosis: What is it?

Good haemostasis is not a problem. However, disease follows irregularities in this process of clot formation and removal – haemorrhage when clots are not formed, and thrombosis when too many or too large a clot is formed too rapidly. Thrombosis can occur in the arteries or in the veins (the latter being a **veno-thromboembolism**, or veno-thromboembolic event, **VTE**).

Thrombosis is more likely to happen in conditions of increased numbers of platelets and high levels of fibrinogen, the inappropriate activation of the entire system, and/or the lack or ineffectiveness of inhibitors. Both high numbers of platelets and raised fibrinogen are present in smoking, hypertension, diabetes and hypercholesterolaemia. These are, of course, the risk factors for arterial thrombosis and atherosclerosis. Obesity is an important modifiable risk factor for VTE.

Clots in the veins (i.e. VTE) are somewhat different to those in arteries; there are more risk factors but the clots are generally in only two places: the legs (where a deep vein thrombosis [DVT] can develop) and the vessels of the lung (where a pulmonary embolus [PE] may arise). Rarely, the subclavian and mesenteric vessels, and the vena cava are burdened. DVT generally includes the large saphenous and femoral veins although some classify calf vein thrombosis separately.

Why are DVT and PE important?

Not only do DVT and PE lead to considerable morbidity, clots also kill!

- A DVT leads to a swollen, painful leg such that walking can be difficult, perhaps impossible. DVTs by themselves are rarely fatal but can produce considerable long-term morbidity. There is also powerful evidence that DVT seeds PE. About two-thirds of all VTEs are DVT.

- Blockage of a crucial lung vessel (be it an artery or a vein) by a PE will lead to breathlessness and pain, can lead in the long term to congestive lung disease and heart disease, and can indeed be fatal. PEs make up about a third of all VTEs.

But how big a problem is VTE and who is likely to suffer an event? In a UK study from the 1980s, about 10% of hospital deaths (1% of admissions) were attributable to PE (Sandler and Martin, 1989). However, lower limb DVT has been documented in 50% of major orthopaedic operations performed without anti-thrombotic prophylaxis, in 25% of patients with acute myocardial infarction and in more than 50% of acute ischaemic stroke cases.

VTE is far from a benign condition; ten years after thrombosis:

- Over half will have suffered **post-thrombotic syndrome**. This is a late consequence of DVT. Clinical signs are chronic leg pain, cramps, varicose veins, redness, swelling, eczema, dermatitis etc., and often follows valve destruction. Leg ulcers (present in 0.2% of the general population) are observed in 2–10% of patients 10 years after their first symptomatic DVT.

- Over a quarter will have suffered a recurrent VTE.

- Over a quarter will be dead: mostly from cancer, congestive lung disease, myocardial infarction or stroke.

Consolidation   *(see pages 93–96 for answers)*

1.1 What are the two major constituents of a clot?

1.2 What are the two major coagulation factors in the blood?

1.3 What is the name for the process of clot destruction?

1.4 What product of clot destruction can be measured in the plasma?

Chapter 2

Who is at risk of these conditions and why?

The many causes of DVT and PE can be divided into two groups: those which are hereditary and those which are acquired. A clear clinical risk factor for thrombosis can often be identified in over 80% of patients, but there is often more than one factor at play in a given patient.

Most common risk factors for DVT and PE

Increasing age

Epidemiology studies suggest a rate of 100 per 100,000 people (0.1%) per year in the general population that translates to some 55,000 cases in the UK annually. This rate is strongly influenced by age: < 5 per 100,000 teenagers, 30 per 100,000 in 25 to 35-year-olds, to 500 per 100,000 80-year-olds (White, 2003). This may be due to immobility and/or coagulopathy.

Major general surgery

The risk of VTE after major general surgery has been extensively documented – it generally includes abdominal or thoracic surgery requiring general anaesthesia of over 30 minutes. Examples of this include coronary artery bypass grafting, surgery for gynaecological malignancies and major urological surgery.

Major orthopaedic surgery and other bone trauma

Lower extremity orthopaedic operations such as total hip and knee replacement carry a particularly high risk and without prophylaxis, about 50% develop VTE. Arthroscopy is of particularly low risk, so that prophylaxis is optional, dependent on other risk factors. VTE is common in fracture of the pelvis, hip or long bones.

Indeed, in one of the first trials of an anticoagulant, the incidence of death from PE after hip fracture fell from 10% to zero!

Cancer

VTE is a frequent complication in patients with cancer and represents a common clinical problem, often preceding diagnosis of cancer by months or years. In the past, patients with cancer were nearly twice as likely to die of PE as those with benign disease and about 60% of these deaths occur prematurely. In one community study the one-year survival of those with cancer and a VTE was 12%, compared to 36% in those with cancer but no VTE (Sørenson et al., 2000).

Patients with cancer represent maybe 15–20% of all new cases of VTE occurring in the community. Conversely, perhaps 10% of people with idiopathic VTEs are ultimately diagnosed with cancer within the year, and appear to be particularly predominant in lymphoma, carcinoma of the pancreas, ovary, breast, lung, brain, pelvis, rectum and gastrointestinal tract.

Therapeutic interventions in patients with cancer, especially surgery and chemotherapy (such as cytotoxic drugs) further increase the risk for thrombosis. Unfortunately, there are few standardised protocols for the management of patients with cancer and the approaches vary.

Pregnancy, the puerperium and synthetic hormones

The incidence of VTE in healthy young women not taking an oral contraceptive pill (OCP) is about 0.5 to 1 per 10,000 per year. Use of a low-dose OCP gives a 3- to 5-fold risk increase (e.g. to 2.5 per 10,000). Almost all these VTEs are DVT, and so are rarely fatal.

Pregnancy increases VTE risk considerably (i.e. to 5 in 10,000). PE is a leading cause of death after childbirth, with 10 events per 10,000 births, although only one of these is likely to be fatal. The risk of DVT following childbirth rises to 20 times that of age-matched non-pregnant women, and is raised even higher by smoking and a history of previous VTE.

The risk of VTE in hormone replacement therapy (HRT) is 2- to 4-fold compared to age matched controls. Women with a history of VTE who are using HRT are at greater risk of recurrence than those not on HRT. Interestingly, men on oestrogens for prostate cancer are also at an increased risk of VTE. A note on practical aspects of risk. Suppose the risk of a DVT on one type of OCP is 15 per 100,000. This translates to one woman getting a VTE from 6,667 women on that pill. Whether or not this risk is acceptable depends on the woman!

The frequency of these and other risk factors are presented in Table 2.1.

Table 2.1 Risk factors in 1,231 patients with VTE
Adapted from Anderson and Wheeler, 1992

Risk factor	%	Risk factor	%
Age > 40 years	88.5	Obesity	37.8
History of VTE	26.0	Cancer	22.3
Bed rest > 5 days	12.0	Major surgery	11.2
Congestive heart failure	8.2	Varicose veins	5.8
Hip or leg fracture	3.7	Oestrogen use	2.0
Stroke	1.8	Multiple trauma	1.1
Childbirth	1.1	Myocardial infarction	0.7

One or more risks was present in 96% of subjects,
two or more risks in 76%, and three or more risks in 39%

Thrombophilia

A separate condition has been described for the appearance of a VTE in 20% of people who lack a clear risk factor (i.e. those above). This condition is called **thrombophilia** (literally, clot loving), and is typically suspected in a slim young woman not on the oral contraceptive pill whose clot appears 'out of the blue', especially if she has a family history of VTE. The most common reasons for thrombophilia are genetic (Table 2.2).

Factor V Leiden is the most common genetic cause of unexplained VTE, and has a remarkable evolutionary history. In its heterozygous state it is prevalent in about 5% of the population of North-West Europe, North America, Australia, (white) South Africa and New Zealand, with lesser incidence in India and Pakistan and in some black populations in Africa. It leads to a seven-fold increase in the risk of VTE and is present in about 20% of unselected, consecutive patients with DVT.

Table 2.2 Prevalence of inherited risk factors for VTE in Caucasians

Risk factor	Prevalence in the general population (%)	Prevalence in patients with VTE
Factor V Leiden	5	High
Prothrombin gene mutation	2	Moderate
Protein S deficiency	0.7	Low
Protein C deficiency	0.2–0.4	Low
Antithrombin deficiency	0.02	Low

Other contributors to thrombophilia include high coagulation Factor VIII, and **antiphospholipid antibodies**. Many such conditions are hereditary, so family history may be relevant. Therefore thrombosis can occur if there is a problem not simply with excess generation of a clot, but also with the lack of inhibitors (Proteins C and S, anti-thrombin) that would normally limit the development of such a thrombosis. These problems compound in the rare and unfortunate persons who lack more than one inhibitor. Thus those with dual Factor V Leiden and anti-thrombin deficiency are at very high risk of thrombosis.

However, not all VTE risk factors are equal: some are more dangerous than others (see below). Furthermore, the risk of VTE is often additive in the presence of several risk factors. One research paper reported an increased risk of VTE of 2.4 times in the obese (BMI > 30). A combination of obesity and Factor V Leiden brings a risk of 7.9 times. However, the risk of VTE in an obese woman using oral contraceptives is 23.8 times that of a normal BMI woman not on the pill.

Risk factor stratification

- **Strong risk factors (increased risk > 10)**
  Hip, pelvis or leg fracture, hip or knee replacement, major general surgery (e.g. CABG), major trauma, spinal cord injury.

- **Moderate risk factors (increased risk 2–9)**
  Arthroscopic knee surgery, central venous lines, malignancy (alone, 4 times, but with chemotherapy this rises to 6 times), congestive heart or respiratory failure,

HRT, use of oral contraceptives, paralytic stroke, pregnancy (post-partum), previous VTE, thrombophilia.

- **Weak risk factors (increased risk < 2)**
  Bed rest > 3 days, immobility due to sitting (e.g. prolonged car or air travel, wheelchair), increasing age, laparoscopic surgery (e.g. cholecystectomy), obesity, pregnancy (ante-partum), varicose veins.

Consolidation   *(see pages 93–96 for answers)*

2.1 Describe some surgical procedures that carry a strong risk of DVT or PE

2.2 Which risk factors are relevant only to women?

2.3 Why do some risk factors seem to promote thrombosis?

2.4 What genetic condition is the most common cause of thrombophilia?

Chapter 3

Recognising and confirming VTE

Almost all VTEs are either DVT or PE (and sometimes both). Diagnosis of VTE based on clinical observation alone is of poor accuracy: in DVT it is correct in only 25 to 33% of cases. However, other aids are available: compression ultrasonography and contrast venography for DVT, ventilation perfusion scan for PE, and the blood test D-dimers for both types of VTE.

Recognising DVT

Clinical signs

The problem is with the presenting patient. What is the problem? It may not be a DVT. Possible non-DVT causes of pain or swelling of the leg include:

- Superficial phlebitis, post-thrombotic syndrome, chronic venous insufficiency and venous obstruction.

- Cellulitis, Baker's cyst, torn gastrocnemius muscle, fracture, haematoma, acute arterial ischaemia, lymphoedema and hypoproteinaemia (for example, cirrhosis).

As only a minority of patients (estimated to be 25 to 33%) presenting with a suspected DVT actually have the condition, a reliable algorithm for differential diagnosis is needed.

DVT commonly presents with pain, erythema, tenderness and swelling of the affected limb. Findings on examination include a palpable cord (reflecting a thrombosed vein), warmth, oedema or superficial venous dilatation. Non-deep veins include those of the calf. Objective diagnosis of DVT (as with PE) is important for best management, and although clinical diagnosis is imprecise, models based on clinical features are fairly practical and reliable in predicting the likelihood of an event.

Imaging

Compression ultrasonography remains the non-invasive tool of choice for the investigation and diagnosis of clinically suspected DVT. Although such imaging is highly sensitive for detecting proximal (groin [iliac] and upper leg [saphenous]) DVT, it is less accurate in the case of isolated DVT of the calf. The ideal method, invasive contrast angiography, is used when a definitive answer is required. Newer imaging techniques being developed (for example, magnetic resonance venography, computed tomography) could detect pelvic vein thromboses although further testing is necessary to establish their role in the diagnosis of DVT.

D-dimers

This blood test adds to the diagnostic accuracy of the non-invasive tests as levels are high in nearly all patients with a VTE. However, several common conditions also lead to raised D-dimers, such as cancer, atherosclerosis, smoking, obesity and diabetes.

Thus, a low or normal D-dimer with a low pre-test probability makes a diagnosis of DVT (or, indeed, of PE) unlikely and therefore excludes this possible diagnosis.

The Wells score for DVT

Adapted from Wells et al., 1997, and Ho et al., 2005

For assessment of pre-test probability of a suspected DVT:

- Score 1 point each for the following: tenderness along the entire deep vein system, swelling of the entire leg, greater than 3 cm difference in calf circumference, pitting oedema, collateral superficial veins, risk factors present (active cancer, prolonged immobility or paralysis, recent surgery or major medical illness).

- Subtract 2 points for an alternative diagnosis likely (e.g. as above: ruptured Baker's cyst in rheumatoid arthritis, superficial thrombophlebitis or infective cellulitis).

- Result: Greater than 3: High probability.
           1–2:   Moderate probability
           0 or less: Low probability

Figure 3.1 shows a practical approach to the diagnosis of DVT using the pre-test probability model, ultrasound, D-dimers and a clinical approach to diagnosis.

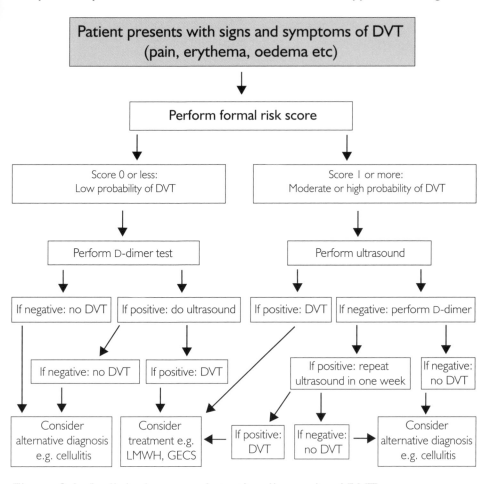

Figure 3.1 A clinical approach to the diagnosis of DVT
Adapted from Aguilar et al., 2002, and Ho et al., 2005

Recognising PE

Those presenting with sudden onset of breathlessness with haemoptysis, pleuritic chest pain, or collapse with shock, in the absence of other causes should be investigated urgently, as PE has a high risk of mortality and morbidity.

Most patients have no leg symptoms at diagnosis, with less than a third having signs or symptoms of a DVT. Conversely, many patients with symptomatic DVT may have asymptomatic PE. Given the common pathophysiology, this is not surprising. Indeed, it has been suggested that 90% of cases arise from asymptomatic DVT.

A similar clinical model to that for DVT has been developed for PE. These consider the most common symptoms of:

- dyspnoea, present in 73%
- pleuritic pain, present in 66%
- cough, present in 37%

and the most common signs of:

- tachypnoea, present in 70%
- crepitations, present in 51%
- tachycardia, present in 30%.

Adapted from Stein et a.l, 1991, and Stein and Henry, 1997. Data from study evaluating clinical characteristics due only to PE. Acute PE present in 117 patients: PE excluded in 248 patients.

In severe PE, circulatory collapse, atrial fibrillation and cardiac arrest may occur. Probably the ultimate diagnostic tool for PE is the ventilation-perfusion (VQ) scan. However, this may not always be available. Accordingly, as for DVT, a scoring system for PE has been devised.

The Wells score for PE
Adapted from Wells et al., 2001, and Lee et al., 2005

- Score 3 points for each of clinical features of DVT and no alternative explanation for acute breathlessness or pleuritic chest pain.

- Score 1.5 points for each of recent prolonged immobility or surgery in the previous 4 weeks, previous history of DVT or PE, and resting heart rate > 100 bpm.

- Score 1 point for each of active cancer and haemoptysis.

- Result: Greater than 6.0: High probability
          2.0–6.0:   Moderate probability
          1.5 or less: Low probability

Measurement of D-dimer levels, as used for DVT, is helpful, especially when combined with other markers. Figure 3.2 shows a practical approach to the diagnosis of PE using a number of factors: the pre-test probability model, imaging, the laboratory, and a clinical approach to diagnosis, although others exist.

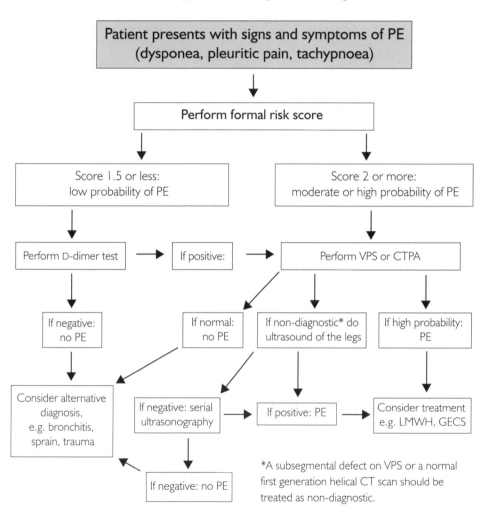

VPS = ventilation perfusion scan, CTPA = computed tomography pulmonary angiogram.

Figure 3.2 A clinical approach to the diagnosis of PE
Adapted from Chunilal and Ginsberg, 2000, and Lee et al., 2005

Consolidation

(see pages 93–96 for answers)

3.1 What are the most common clinical signs and symptoms of DVT?

3.2 What other aids are there to help diagnosis?

3.3 What are the most common signs and symptoms of PE?

3.4 What other aids are there to help a diagnosis?

Case Study 1 *For answers see pages 96–98*

A 65-year-old woman with type II diabetes and a body mass index of 32.9 presents to A&E with a 24-hour history of pain, tenderness and swelling in the left leg. The circumference of the left calf is 2 cm greater than the right. Chest sounds are normal and she has no pain or cough. Blood pressure is 123/76 mmHg, pulse rate 77 bpm. A venous blood sample is obtained and sent to the laboratory, with the result of no evidence of systemic inflammation. However, the level of D-dimers is raised at 750 units/mL (normal range <500 units/mL).

What action would you take?

Chapter 4

What have we got to treat these conditions?

Clearly, step one to reducing the risk of thrombosis is to address the pathological risk factors (e.g. diabetes). However, in practice, this is often difficult, and we fall back on medicines. Although clotting involves platelet activation, VTE prevention and treatment is generally aimed at clotting proteins like fibrinogen. There are two families: oral (warfarin and phenidione [generic]) and **parenteral** (heparins and hirudins). However, there are also non-drug treatments. A key reference book for all drugs is the *British National Formulary (BNF)*. This important book not only lists drugs, but also gives indications, interactions and doses.

Oral anticoagulants

Warfarin

Vitamin K, normally obtained in our diet, is an essential requirement in our ability to synthesise key molecules involved in coagulation, so if we are deficient in this vitamin (by diet or by poison), we can't make them as efficiently and so don't clot that efficiently.

Warfarin, the most widely used anticoagulant in the UK and western world, is a slow poison that specifically blocks the liver's production of vitamin K-dependent prothrombin and Factors VII and X, protein C and protein S. Thus, in the laboratory and in the body, clotting takes longer to happen. This leads, in real terms, to a protection from thrombosis.

Use of warfarin demands frequent laboratory monitoring. Patient's prothrombin time is compared to normal plasma, to produce the **International Normalised Ratio (INR)**. The degree of anticoagulation required varies on clinical circumstance but target INR usually ranges from 2 to 4. Because warfarin has a narrow therapeutic index, changes in health or concurrent medication require more intensive monitoring of the INR.

The INR is simply the ratio between the times that whole blood or plasma (i.e. the **prothrombin time**) takes to clot normally, compared to the (supposedly increased) time it takes to clot due to warfarin. We use the INR to strike a balance between slowing down the clot-forming process, and the use of too much warfarin, which will interfere with clotting to such an extent that a clot may never happen.

Phenindione and acenocoumarol

These are alternative oral vitamin K antagonists for those unwilling or unable to tolerate warfarin. However, concerns regarding the potential for hepatotoxicity, nephrotoxicity and other blood problems have reduced their role largely to those allergic to, intolerant of, or hypersensitive to warfarin.

Parenteral treatments

Heparin

This natural anticoagulant's major effect is accounted for by its support for anti-thrombin in the (obvious) inactivation of thrombin but also coagulation Factor Xa (and some others). The short half-life means that it must be given continuously, and it must be given parenterally (through the skin), preferably by continuous IV infusion (i.e. a pump) and is therefore inappropriate for home use. The effect of heparin on the clotting cascade must be monitored in the laboratory by measuring the **activated partial thromboplastin time (APTT)**, generally aiming for an **APTT ratio** of 1.5 to 2.5 times that of control. This system is a rough parallel to the use of the INR for warfarin treatment.

The proven efficacy of heparin in numerous settings (e.g. DVT, in acute coronary syndromes) must, like that of warfarin, be set against adverse effects. These include haemorrhage, osteoporosis, alopecia, and hypersensitivity. However, probably the most important is a low platelet count, perhaps less than 100×10^9/L, and certainly less than 50×10^9/L, i.e. thrombocytopenia. Hence this heparin-induced thrombocytopenia (HIT), which happens in perhaps 1–3% of patients on this drug, can compound a bleeding event and even cause a thrombosis. If this happens then the heparin must be stopped and an alternative anticoagulant provided (generally, a hirudin, see below). A second major problem is a risk of hyperkalaemia, so serum potassium measurement may be advisable.

Heparin is available as a non-proprietary drug, but also as tradenames Calciparine, Monoparin, Monoparin Calcium, and Multiparin. 'Old-fashioned' **unfractionated heparin (UFH)** is quite crude structurally, and about 15 years ago was 'cleaned up' into a new preparation.

Low Molecular Weight Heparin (LMWH)

Recently, this safer form of heparin has been introduced. Although it also cannot be taken orally, it is safe enough to be given by one-off injection, even in out-patients and at home, and does not need to be monitored in the laboratory by the APTT test. A further good point is that there is also a reduced incidence of side effects such as osteoporosis and HIT. The differences between the old style unfractionated heparin and the newer LMWHs are outlined in Table 4.1.

In those few cases where monitoring is deemed necessary (e.g. to test the effective dose in prophylaxis of VTE in high-risk pregnancy), laboratory measurement of plasma levels of anti-Factor Xa activity is required. Tests of APTT are unhelpful.

The British National Formulary (September 2008) lists four different types of LMWH:

- Bemiparin (Zibor)
- Dalteparin (Fragmin)
- Enoxaparin (Clexane)
- Tinzaparin (Innohep).

These commercial preparations vary in the licences that they have been granted for use in different clinical conditions, but also in the ratio of anti-Xa to anti-thrombin activity, although the clinical relevance of this is uncertain. Also listed is the heparinoid called Danaparoid (Orgaran).

Table 4.1 Comparison of LMWH and unfractionated heparin

	Unfractionated Heparin	LMWH
Action	Anti-thrombin, Factor Xa, and others	Almost completely anti-Xa
Route of administration	Subcutaneous or intravenous	Subcutaneous
Subcutaneous adsorption	Slow	Improved
Protein-binding	Proteins in plasma and on endothelium	Reduced protein binding so more effective
Approx. mol. weight	15,000	4,000–6,000
Effective half-life	Subcutaneous: 1.5 hours Intravenous: 30 minutes	4 hours
Between and within individual variation	Extensive	Minimal
Monitoring	APPT	If required, anti-Xa activity
Elimination	Liver and kidney: so failure of both organs is important	Kidney: so renal function must be considered

Other anticoagulants

Fondaparinux

Fondaparinux is a novel, selective and reversible Xa-inhibitor, which although based on the structure of heparin, is different from both heparin and LMWH. Pharmacokinetics are characterised by a 100% bioavailability by subcutaneous route, lack of biometabolism, urinary excretion and a relatively long plasma half-life of 14 to 21 hours.

There is a rapid onset of action, with a peak activity reached in 2 hours. No interactions with aspirin, warfarin or digitoxin have been noted.

Fondaparinux, like LMWHs, does not affect the prothrombin time (PT) and has very weak effects on APPT but its activity can be determined by specific anti-Xa assays, if necessary. Thrombocytopenia (platelet count $< 100 \times 10^9$/L) occurs even less commonly than with LMWH.

Hirudins

These small anticoagulant peptides, purified from the leech *Hirudo medicinalis*, bind thrombin with high specificity and sensitivity. With a true half-life of about an hour, the half-life effect on the APTT is 2 to 3 hours. Consequently it may be seen as a competitor to heparin in several indications such as HIT and unstable angina. Examples include Hirulog, Argatroban, Desirudin, Lepirudin and Bivalirudin (see the BNF).

Dextran

This polysaccharide is cumbersome and may give rise to adverse effects, so is rarely used. See the BNF for additional details on all agents.

Dabigatran

Dabigatran (also called Pradaxa) is a new thrombin inhibitor that has recently (Spring 2008, so may not be in old editions of the BNF) been licensed for the primary prevention of VTE in adults who have undergone a total hip or knee replacement. A great strength of this new drug, which is likely to be a competitor for LMWH and warfarin, is that it can be given orally (like warfarin but unlike LMWH)) but does not need to be monitored in the laboratory (like LMWH but unlike warfarin or unfractionated heparin). However, like these other anticoagulants, caution is advised in patients with liver or renal disease.

Non-drug treatments

General measures

As immobility increases the risk of DVT about ten-fold, early mobilisation and leg exercises to reduce stasis should be encouraged in all patients as much as is practicable. Similarly, as haemoconcentration increases blood viscosity and reduces blood flow, adequate hydration should be ensured in all patients.

Inferior vena cava filters

The key document in this section is the guideline on the use of vena cava filters (VCFs) published in the *British Journal of Haematology* (2006) by the British Committee for Standards in Haematology (see www.bschguidelines.com).

If (some say 'when') DVT in the legs embolise and clots pass up the vena cava, they may ultimately end up in the lung and so cause a PE. One way to prevent formation of PE is to physically prevent these small thrombi from reaching the lung by placing a filter in the inferior vena cava (hence VCF) often at a level just below the renal veins. From the technical point of view, VCFs are best placed with assistance from ultrasound and fluoroscopy, quite probably by an interventional radiologist. The use of VCFs focuses on:

● patients who have a contraindication to anticoagulation

● pregnant women who develop VTE shortly before delivery (whether or not they have a contraindication for anticoagulation)

● selected patients with PE despite therapeutic anticoagulation, although these patients may benefit from high dose warfarin (target INR 3.5) or LMWH prior to VCF placement, particularly in patients with thrombophilia or cancer

● selected patients with PE despite therapeutic anticoagulation.

VCFs are not indicated in unselected patients with VTE who receive conventional pharmacotherapy, in those undergoing thrombolysis, or in those with free-floating thrombus. However, it is common practice to initiate anticoagulation after VCF placement if and when there is no longer a contraindication to anticoagulation. Although VCFs have been shown to reduce the occurrence of new PEs, curiously, they also bring a risk of new DVT. This happened despite the use of anticoagulant therapy. Early complications of VCF placement include insertion-site thrombosis and infection. Late complications include recurrent DVT, inferior vena cava thrombosis and post-thrombotic syndrome.

Thus the decision to introduce anticoagulant therapy in a patient with a VCF should be based on the perceived underlying risk of the condition and the likelihood of anti-coagulant therapy-based bleeding.

Mechanical methods

Graduated elastic compression stockings (GECS) are effective in prophylaxis of asymptomatic DVT and symptomatic PE in surgical patients (n.b. suspender also available). GECS are available in above- and below-knee but the former are preferred for DVT prophylaxis. However, there can be problems with GECS and certainly not all patients can tolerate them (see Table 5.5, p. 40).

Intermittent Pneumatic Compression (IPC) devices periodically compress the calf and/or thigh muscles with an inflation pressure of 35–40 mmHg for about 10 seconds to a minute. They are generally applied immediately before or during surgery, are effective in prophylaxis of asymptomatic DVT in surgical patients, and are often subsequently replaced by GECS. Other mechanical and surgical treatments (e.g. **embolectomy**) are usually reserved for massive life-threatening PE where drug treatments have failed or are contraindicated.

Thrombolytic therapy (getting rid of the clot)

Unlike heparins and warfarin (that antagonise extension and recurrence of thrombosis), thrombolytic agents (e.g. streptokinase, urokinase, alteplase, reteplase – collectively called tissue plasminogen activators – tPA) actually lyse the thrombi. However, indications for this therapy are unclear. Recent guidelines do not recommend thrombolysis or thrombectomy for DVT unless there is danger of the limb being lost (i.e. amputated).

Notably, these drugs are also used to treat the symptoms of acute myocardial infarction – i.e. the chest pain that is presumed to be the result of a thrombus in one of the coronary arteries. In acute PE these treatments (e.g. alteplase 50 mg) are reserved for the most serious and unstable cases, where there is haemodynamic instability. Thrombolytic therapy infusion into the pulmonary artery (after clot disruption using a pigtail catheter manipulated within the pulmonary artery) has been reported. As discussed, a VCF may be considered.

Anti-platelet therapy

Almost all patients should be able to tolerate oral or parenteral anticoagulant, but for those who cannot (for whatever reason), anti-platelet drugs **aspirin** and **clopidogrel** (Plavix) are an alternative. However, it is established that anti-platelet drugs are not as effective in reducing the risk of VTE as are anticoagulant drugs. Anti-platelet therapy is leading choice for the treatment of arterial thrombosis.

Consolidation

(see pages 93–96 for answers)

4.1 How does warfarin work?

4.2 How do we monitor the effect of warfarin on the blood?

4.3 Can you name any disadvantages of heparin?

4.4 What non-drug treatments are available?

Case Study 2 *For answers see pages 96–98*

A 69-year-old woman has elective hip-replacement surgery. Her recovery is good and she is maintained after her operation with analgesia and unfractionated heparin. However, after a week she starts to suffer nosebleeds and her wound begins to ooze. A blood test for her heparin reveals an APTT ratio of 2.1 (desired result between 1.5 and 2.5) but a platelet count of 75×10^9 cells/mL (desired range between 140 and 400).

What has happened and what do you need to do?

Chapter 5

Clinical practice of anticoagulation

These pharmaceutical agents can be dangerous and must be used with care – overuse can lead to life-terminating haemorrhage. However, there are numerous guidelines about how to use these drugs in different clinical settings. Many such guidelines are based on books and published research papers, many of which are available on the internet, and many are free.

● Perhaps the most accessible is the *British National Formulary (BNF)*, widely available in NHS hospitals and regularly updated (see www.bnf.org).

● The British Committee on Standardisation in Haematology (BCSH) offers reasonably up-to-date guidelines for out-patient treatment of DVT with warfarin or heparin at www.bcshguidelines.com. These are downloadable free.

Local practice and management

The House of Commons Health Committee report *The Prevention of Thromboembolism in Hospitalised Patients* (The Stationery Office 2005) recommends that each hospital establish a '**Thrombosis Committee**'. There is the clear implication that this committee will co-ordinate and issue local guidelines.

The UK national guideline-setting body, **National Institute for Health and Clinical Excellence (NICE)**, released its *Document 46* in April 2007, devoted to reducing the risk of thrombosis after surgery. Other NICE guidelines will follow in 2009 on the use of anticoagulants in medical patients. Another body, the **National Patient Safety Agency (NPSA)** has released its own guidelines on the management of the patient on warfarin.

A Trust or other body undertaking anticoagulation is required to set its own internal guidelines, based on documents such as those from NICE and the NPSA, which may not apply to another Trust, PCT, General Practice or, indeed, Practitioner. Therefore...

Statement

What follows is informed comment and **NOT** guidelines

NO responsibility is taken for their use in clinical practice

Practitioners are expected to refer to their own Trust Guidelines

---

Most in-patients (surgical or medical) are likely to be at a relatively high and acute risk of thrombosis. In which case they are likely to be treated with LMWH. However, it is also possible that some patients will come into hospital already taking warfarin. If so, this may need to be reduced or stopped altogether. Patients may also benefit from GECS. In many cases the risk of thrombosis will still be present after the patient is fit for discharge. If this is the case then the patient is likely to be discharged with GECS and treated with warfarin as an out-patient. The latter will most likely be commenced on the ward.

Patients may also be referred for anticoagulation (perhaps by a Trust colleague or by a General Practitioner) whilst not at immediate acute risk of thrombosis (i.e. with newly-diagnosed atrial fibrillation).

The text that follows will adopt this general scheme. The immediate clinical questions will be suggestions relevant to prophylaxis with LMWH in medical and surgical in-patients. As in many cases the risk of thrombosis will extend beyond the patient's stay in hospital, then prophylaxis with warfarin will become necessary. Comments regarding the use of warfarin will therefore follow those for the use of LMWH. Flowchart 5.1 illustrates these issues.

Risk Assessment for treatment with LMWH

ALL in-patients (regardless of medical/surgical indication) **MUST** be assessed for the risk of developing VTE to identify those at highest risk and to identify any contraindications to thromboprophylaxis. The practitioner will identify specific risk factors (introduced in Table 2.1), as some risk factors are more dangerous than others, and prepare a total score as follows:

Table 5.1 Risk factors for VTE

RISK FACTORS (SCORE 1)	RISK FACTORS (SCORE 2)	RISK FACTORS (SCORE 3)
Age > 60	Oestrogen-containing pill	Immobile (> 72 hours)
Obesity (BMI > 30)	HRT	History of DVT/PE
IHD, CCF or previous stroke	Known thrombophilic conditions	
Significant COPD	Malignancy	
Extensive varicose veins	Sepsis	
Inflammatory bowel disease	Known family history in 2 relatives (at least 1 first degree)	
Nephrotic syndrome	Pregnancy (post-partum)	
Myeloproliferative disorders	Pregnancy (ante-partum)	

BMI = body mass index; IHD = ischaemic heart disease;
CCF = congestive cardiac failure; HRT = hormone replacement therapy;
COPD = Chronic obstructive pulmonary disease

For elective admissions for surgery an assessment of risk should take place at the pre-assessment clinic appointment, where appropriate. For all others, the assessment of risk should take place on admission to the ward. Where patients are undergoing surgery, high-risk procedures should be taken into consideration as some procedures are more likely to cause a DVT or PE than are others (Table 5.2).

Often, day surgery patients do not routinely receive anticoagulation, as they are mobile within a few hours postoperatively. However, it is possible that patients at risk of VTE may be admitted as a day case. The suitability of such patients for one dose of LMWH should be discussed with the consultant in charge.

Flowchart 5.1 Anticoagulation management simplified

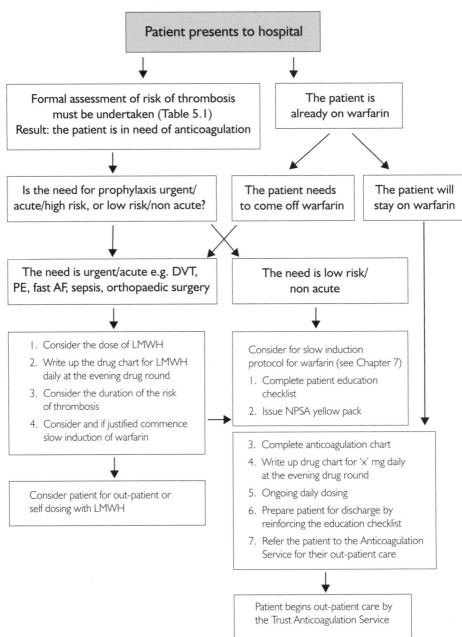

Patient presents to hospital

Formal assessment of risk of thrombosis must be undertaken (Table 5.1) Result: the patient is in need of anticoagulation

The patient is already on warfarin

Is the need for prophylaxis urgent/acute/high risk, or low risk/non acute?

The patient needs to come off warfarin

The patient will stay on warfarin

The need is urgent/acute e.g. DVT, PE, fast AF, sepsis, orthopaedic surgery

The need is low risk/non acute

1. Consider the dose of LMWH
2. Write up the drug chart for LMWH daily at the evening drug round
3. Consider the duration of the risk of thrombosis
4. Consider and if justified commence slow induction of warfarin

Consider for slow induction protocol for warfarin (see Chapter 7)
1. Complete patient education checklist
2. Issue NPSA yellow pack

Consider patient for out-patient or self dosing with LMWH

3. Complete anticoagulation chart
4. Write up drug chart for 'x' mg daily at the evening drug round
5. Ongoing daily dosing
6. Prepare patient for discharge by reinforcing the education checklist
7. Refer the patient to the Anticoagulation Service for their out-patient care

Patient begins out-patient care by the Trust Anticoagulation Service

Table 5.2 Additional risk factors for surgical in-patients

SCORE	SURGICAL PROCEDURE
4	Major trauma; e.g. lower limb fractures
4	Major joint replacement
4	Surgery for fractured neck of femur
3	Thoracotomy or abdominal surgery involving mid-line laparotomy.
3	Total abdominal hysterectomy; including laparoscopic assisted.
2	Intraperitoneal laparoscopic surgery lasting > 30 minutes
2	Vascular surgery (not intra-abdominal)
1	Surgery lasting > 30 minutes
0	Surgery lasting < 30 minutes

The total risk score will give an initial guide to therapy, although LMWH may not be appropriate for all patients. If so, anti-platelet therapy (aspirin ± Plavix) is an option.

Contraindications to heparin and warfarin

After clinical assessment has demonstrated an indication for prophylaxis with heparin or warfarin, the patient's medical and drug history must be assessed for the cautions and contraindications to both agents. These are indicated in Tables 5.3 and 5.4.

Table 5.3 Contraindications and cautions to heparin prophylaxis

CONTRAINDICATIONS	CAUTIONS
Known uncorrected bleeding disorders e.g. haemophilias	Severe hepatic impairment
Severe to moderate thrombocytopenia (seek advice)	Severe renal impairment
Heparin allergy	Major trauma or surgery to the brain, eye or spinal cord.
Heparin-induced thrombocytopenia	
Heparin-induced thrombosis	
Patients on existing anticoagulation therapy	
Bleeding or potentially bleeding lesions, e.g. • Oesophageal varices, active peptic ulcer • Recent intracranial haemorrhage • Intracranial aneurysm or vascular malformation	

Table 5.4 Contraindications and cautions to warfarin prophylaxis

CONTRAINDICATIONS	CAUTIONS
Peptic ulcer, oesophageal varices	Recent surgery or organ biopsy
Severe hypertension (BP >160/100 mmHg)	Alcohol abuse
Thrombocytopenia (platelet count <100 x 10⁹/L)	Previous haemorrhage
Bacterial endocarditis, Cranberry juice	Dementia
Pregnancy*, coagulation disorders	Hepatic impairment (raised LFTs)
Potential bleeding lesions	Renal impairment (raised creatinine)
Poor compliance, clinic attendance	Breast feeding

* Women of child-bearing age taking warfarin should be made aware of the risk of teratogenicity (BNF March 2007).

It follows that for some patients, LMWH or warfarin will not be appropriate. In which case, an alternative is required if the risk of thrombosis is to be reduced. The issues of safety will be recapitulated wherever necessary.

Non-pharmacological treatments

All in-patients will be considered for the use of graduated elastic compression stockings (GECS). However, contraindications and cautions apply. The practitioner will consider these before recommending their use (Table 5.5).

Table 5.5 Contraindications and cautions for the use of GECS

CONTRAINDICATIONS	CAUTIONS
Massive oedema of the legs or pulmonary oedema from congestive heart failure	Select correct size. Apply carefully aligning toe hole under toe
Severe arteriosclerosis or other vascular disease of the leg	Check fitting daily for change in leg circumference
Extreme deformity of the leg	Do not fold down
Local leg condition e.g. dermatitis, gangrene	Remove daily for no more than 30 minutes

Graduated elastic compression stockings may be full-length, thigh-length, or below-knee. Most clinically important DVTs occur above the knee, which provides the rationale for using full-length stockings.

Most controlled studies have used above-knee stockings and the trials comparing above-knee and below-knee stockings have been too small to determine whether or not they are equally effective. This must be balanced by evidence which suggests that below-knee stockings are better tolerated by patients and are easier to apply. All GECS should be prescribed on the drug chart.

The in-patient will be mobilised as much as is practicable, and full attention will be given to adequate hydration.

Treatment

When:

(a) The patient has been assessed and found to be in need of treatment, and
(b) The contraindications or cautions to anticoagulation have been addressed

Then:

(c) The patient must be informed and educated as to the purpose of the particular treatment, and
(d) Treatment can begin according to the following regimes.

1. Acute risk of VTE and no contraindications for LMWH

Table 5.6 Application of risk assessment tables for the use of LMWH

LOW RISK SCORE 0 OR 1	MODERATE RISK SCORE 2 OR 3	HIGH RISK SCORE 4
Early ambulation	GECS	GECS
Consider GECS	Low dose LMWH daily for surgical patients	High dose LMWH daily (max. 14 days for medical in-patients)
	High dose LMWH daily for medical patients	Surgical patients – consider IPC in theatre plus high dose LMWH

Note: For male patients < 57 kg and female patients < 45 kg, caution may be needed regarding the dose of LMWH prescribed. Please consult the clinician in charge of the patient's care. IPC = intermittent pneumatic compression.

2. Acute risk of VTE but contraindications for LMWH

If LMWH is inappropriate then anti-platelet therapy (e.g. enteric coated aspirin 75–300 mg daily or Plavix 75 mg daily) may be considered. Commencement on warfarin may also be considered. However, contraindications to aspirin exist: principally known allergy and gastric erosions.

3. Chronic risk of VTE

The patient will be started on warfarin as an in-patient or as an out-patient (Chapter 7). For example, when considering anticoagulation in the patient with atrial fibrillation:

- Patients at high risk of stroke (e.g. with hypertension, diabetes) should be started on warfarin (target INR 2.0–3.0); if contraindications to warfarin exist (such as bleeding, falls, compliance, concomitant diseases), aspirin 75–300 mg/day should be prescribed.

- Patients at moderate and low risk of stroke should receive aspirin 75–300 mg/day unless contraindicated.

If contraindications to both warfarin and aspirin exist (particularly gastrointestinal bleeding, allergy, etc.), this should be carefully documented in clinical notes and in cases of uncertainty, specialist cardiology referral is needed. Most risk stratification can be performed on clinical criteria. Echocardiography (e.g. for low ejection fraction [< 0.4]) merely refines risk stratification and referral is indicated in situations of uncertainty, based on clinical criteria. Risk stratification should be reviewed at regular intervals, and at least annually.

4. How much LMWH should be given?

This depends on a number of factors. Firstly, the different varieties of LMWH all have different licences for different conditions, such as treatment of proven VTE, or the prevention of VTE that may arise from certain risky situations like orthopaedic surgery (i.e. prophylaxis). LMWHs have different potencies so that the dose from one may be different to the dose from another. Some suggest doses of a certain number of mg, other doses are for a given number of units. Secondly, it may also be the case that doses are different for those in need of treatment of an actual DVT or PE, or in prevention of a possible VTE that may occur in the near future (i.e. prophylaxis after a high risk procedure such as hip replacement).

Prevention (prophylaxis)

The BNF (September 2008), for example, recommends the dose of a particular LMWH for the prophylaxis of DVT in low-risk surgical patients to be 20 mg (2000 units) 2 hours before surgery, then 20 mg every following 24 hours for 7 to10 days. A high risk patient by the same token needs 40 mg (4000 units) 12 hours before surgery and additional 40 mg doses every 24 hours for 7 to 10 days. However, for medical patients, the dose is 40 mg every 24 hours for at least 6 days and until ambulant, to a maximum of 14 days. Doses are fine tuned by indication e.g. orthopaedic surgery or medical admission.

Treatment

However, the same BNF recommends a dose of 1.5mg/kg (150 units/kg) of the same LMWH every 24 hours for the treatment of a proven DVT/PE for at least 5 days and until adequate oral anticoagulation (e.g.warfarin) has been established. So an 80 kg patient may receive 20 mg for prevention, but six times as much (80 x 1.5 = 120 mg) for treatment. At the practical level, this degree of treatment is likely to be of a newly-acquired VTE, often in hospital and therefore as an in-patient. Other LMWHs may have a different dosing regime.

Pregnancy

Here there is a recommendation (although unlicensed) to weight-adjust the dose of LMWH used for treatment of VTE: for weight under 50 kg use 40 mg (4000 units) twice daily, for 50–70 kg use 60 mg (6000 units), for 70–90 kg use 80 mg (8000 units) and for over 90 kg, use 100 mg (10,000 units) – all twice daily.

General points

Also note that doses of some LMWHs may need to be adjusted according to factors such as the weight, body mass index, and renal function (e.g. increased serum creatinine or reduced glomerular filtration rate). Some guidelines may recommend that the dose of LMWH should be that which inhibits Factor Xa to a certain level (i.e. anti-Factor Xa activity). However, other LMWHs may not need to be dosed to this level of precision, and may be given at a standard dose.

It is clear that the role of the Trust's Thrombosis Committee is to guide all practitioners on whichever LMWH best suits their individual requirements. Therefore the practitioner must consult their local guidelines, and recall that these may change from workplace to workplace.

Consolidation   *(see pages 93–96 for answers)*

5.1 Which single document provides details about all anticoagulants?

_____

5.2 What Trust body within your particular workplace should be consulted about best practice?

_____

5.3 What is the basis of the risk factor method for providing treatment?

_____

_____

_____

5.4 Are there patients who should not be given LMWH?

_____

_____

_____

_____

_____

Chapter 6

Use of LMWH

1: General medicine

Most cases of VTE are triggered by causes other than surgery and most fatal PEs occur in medical patients. This group may include patients with:

- Central venous lines, malignancy (greater if on chemotherapy)
- Congestive heart or respiratory failure (including pneumonia)
- HRT, use of oral contraceptives, paralytic stroke
- Pregnancy (post-partum), previous VTE, thrombophilia, bed rest > 3 days
- Immobility due to sitting (e.g. prolonged car or air travel, wheelchair)
- Increasing age, obesity, pregnancy (ante-partum), varicose veins (see Table 5.1).

The following pathway is to be followed in each newly-admitted patient:

1. There must be an assessment to decide whether or not thromboprophylaxis is indicated (Table 5.1).
2. The patient must be assessed for contraindications to LMWH (Table 2.3) and to GECS (Table 5.5).
3. If appropriate, the patient will then be treated and administered with LMWH as follows:

- *Low-risk patients*   – Early mobilisation
                                     – Attention to hydration
                                     – Consider GECS.

- *Moderate-/high-risk patients*   – Early mobilisation
                                     – Attention to hydration
                                     – LMWH s/c daily at 1800 hrs
                                     – GECS

Flowchart 6.1 Algorithm for General Medicine

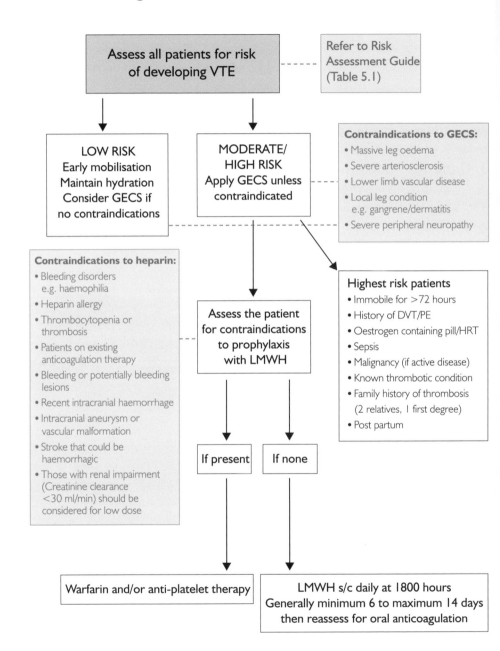

Assess all patients for risk of developing VTE

Refer to Risk Assessment Guide (Table 5.1)

LOW RISK
Early mobilisation
Maintain hydration
Consider GECS if no contraindications

MODERATE/ HIGH RISK
Apply GECS unless contraindicated

Contraindications to GECS:
- Massive leg oedema
- Severe arteriosclerosis
- Lower limb vascular disease
- Local leg condition e.g. gangrene/dermatitis
- Severe peripheral neuropathy

Contraindications to heparin:
- Bleeding disorders e.g. haemophilia
- Heparin allergy
- Thrombocytopenia or thrombosis
- Patients on existing anticoagulation therapy
- Bleeding or potentially bleeding lesions
- Recent intracranial haemorrhage
- Intracranial aneurysm or vascular malformation
- Stroke that could be haemorrhagic
- Those with renal impairment (Creatinine clearance <30 ml/min) should be considered for low dose

Assess the patient for contraindications to prophylaxis with LMWH

Highest risk patients
- Immobile for >72 hours
- History of DVT/PE
- Oestrogen containing pill/HRT
- Sepsis
- Malignancy (if active disease)
- Known thrombotic condition
- Family history of thrombosis (2 relatives, 1 first degree)
- Post partum

If present   If none

Warfarin and/or anti-platelet therapy

LMWH s/c daily at 1800 hours
Generally minimum 6 to maximum 14 days then reassess for oral anticoagulation

4. Those patients intolerant of LMWH will need an alternative such as warfarin (probably target INR 2–3), aspirin (75–300 mg daily) and/or clopidogrel (75 mg daily) in addition to GECS. Note that anti-platelet drugs are regarded as a treatment of last resort only in those patients unable to take anticoagulant drugs. Notably, this is the reverse of the treatment and prevention of arterial thrombosis (heart attack and stroke) where anti-platelet drugs are far more effective than anticoagulant drugs.

Mechanical methods of prophylaxis have not to date been appropriately evaluated in acutely ill medical patients, and thus are not recommended at present.

All information will be recorded in the patients' medical notes.

2: Acute cardiovascular emergencies

The two conditions under this umbrella are post myocardial infarction (acute coronary syndrome) and cerebrovascular event (CVA, stroke). The former is specifically under the care of a cardiologist and more specific guidelines will apply. Similarly, treatment of acute stroke will also be under the close control of stroke physicians who will have their own guidelines. Practitioners are therefore likely to be involved in the anticoagulation of these groups under close scrutiny and closely structured guidelines.

Acute coronary syndromes (ACS)

In the initial management (e.g. in A&E, CCU) patients with an ACS are likely (in the absence of contraindications) to be given aspirin 300 mg followed by 150 mg daily and are also likely to have clopidogrel 75 mg daily after a loading dose of 300 mg. Weight adjusted LMWH (12 hourly) is started ASAP after initial assessment and continued for 3 days (and at least 24 hours after last documented ischaemic episode). For high risk patients other anti-platelet drugs may be indicated. As before, contraindications include abnormal bleeding or stroke within 30 days, haemorrhagic stroke at any time, intracranial disease, severe hypertension (> 160/110 mmHg), increased PT, APTT, or thrombocytopenia.

For subsequent management (inevitably in CCU), cardiologists are likely to consider/plan early coronary angiography (during the same admission) in patients who are candidates for revascularisation. Those with refractory symptoms, post-infarction angina, haemodynamic or rhythm instability require angiography as soon as possible. LMWH is likely to be omitted for at least 8 to 12 hours prior to angiography if planned.

If percutaneous coronary intervention (PCI) angiography demonstrates that angioplasty with possible stenting is appropriate, the procedure should ideally be carried out immediately (in the same session) if feasible providing the patient is fully informed of the potential risk/benefit, or as soon as possible during the same admission. Patients undergoing PCI are likely to receive a reduced dose weight-adjusted bolus of UFH (30–70 u/kg) as well as other drugs so that no further heparin should be given following the procedure (unless specified by the operator). All patients receiving coronary stents should also receive clopidogrel 300 mg (if not already started) following the procedure, followed by 75 mg daily for a year (in addition to aspirin 75 mg daily).

Stroke

The two different types of stroke each demand a completely different approach. Clearly, the haemorrhagic stroke is all about the patient having had a bleed into their brain, so the approach will be to minimise this bleeding. One method undergoing clinical trials is to provide an infusion of coagulation Factor VII to help the formation of a thrombus that aims to prevent the bleed getting worse.

In the alternative, a thrombotic stroke, the emphasis is on removing the clot and so starting revascularisation (as in an acute myocardial infarction). This may be possible by infusion of a tissue plasminogen activator (such as alteplase [NICE guidance June 2007] to help dissolve the clot. An alternative is to try to remove the clot with a special catheter. Post-stroke, it may be necessary to use anti-coagulation to reduce the risk of an additional thrombosis, alongside addressing the risk factors for VTE.

3: Surgery

n.b. *NICE Guideline 46 applies*

Almost all patients will qualify for prophylaxis with low dose LMWH daily at 1800 hours the evening before surgery unless prophylaxis is contraindicated (see Table 5.3) and the patient has been identified as at highest risk of developing VTE. In this case a dose of high dose LMWH daily at 1800 hours should be prescribed. (Flowchart 6.2).

The Independent Expert Working Group that reported to the Chief Medical Officer recommended that aspirin is not recommended for surgical patients (Department of Health, 2007). Clearly, if the patient is intolerant of LMWH then anti-platelets or warfarin are the remaining options.

It is presumed that for elective surgery there has been full laboratory work-up with FBC, U&Es, LFTs etc. If the patient is already on warfarin, refer to Chapter 7.

A. Patients admitted the day(s) before surgery (Flowchart 6.2)

Whenever possible prophylaxis with a high dose of LMWH should be commenced at 1800 hours on the evening before surgery. This will achieve effective prophylaxis combined with minimal additional risk of bleeding complications at the time of regional anaesthesia (e.g. epidural or spinal) and surgery. Thereafter, low dose LMWH (more if at highest risk) should be continued at 1800 hours daily at the same time until anticoagulation with warfarin has reached its target INR, or (in the case of minimal surgery in the young) until the risk of thromboembolism is considered to be minimal.

For patients undergoing transurethral resection of prostate (TURP), low dose LMWH should be given on the evening before surgery (e.g. 1800 hours) unless contraindicated. Postoperative doses should be given as moderate or high risk as normal.

B. Patients admitted on the day of surgery

Patients eligible for prophylaxis should ideally receive a low dose of LMWH two hours pre-operatively, unless this is contraindicated. One of the main contraindi-cations is that the patient is due to be receiving regional anaesthesia (spinal or epidural). See Section D below.

Therefore, if a general anaesthetic only is to be administered, the pre-operative dose should be prescribed by the anaesthetist following the assessment. Patients should then receive a further low dose of LMWH at 1800 hours on the evening following the surgery, for elective admission those who have attended pre-operative assessment, this should have been already prescribed at the clinic.

Thereafter a daily low dose of LMWH at 1800 hours should be prescribed, unless the patient is identified at highest risk when high dose LMWH should be given.

Flowchart 6.2 General algorithm for surgical patients admitted the day before their operation

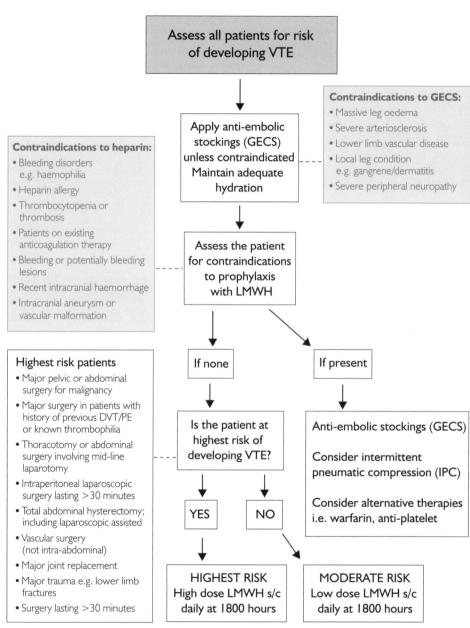

Assess all patients for risk of developing VTE

Contraindications to GECS:
- Massive leg oedema
- Severe arteriosclerosis
- Lower limb vascular disease
- Local leg condition
  e.g. gangrene/dermatitis
- Severe peripheral neuropathy

Apply anti-embolic stockings (GECS) unless contraindicated
Maintain adequate hydration

Contraindications to heparin:
- Bleeding disorders
  e.g. haemophilia
- Heparin allergy
- Thrombocytopenia or thrombosis
- Patients on existing anticoagulation therapy
- Bleeding or potentially bleeding lesions
- Recent intracranial haemorrhage
- Intracranial aneurysm or vascular malformation

Assess the patient for contraindications to prophylaxis with LMWH

Highest risk patients
- Major pelvic or abdominal surgery for malignancy
- Major surgery in patients with history of previous DVT/PE or known thrombophilia
- Thoracotomy or abdominal surgery involving mid-line laparotomy
- Intraperitoneal laparoscopic surgery lasting >30 minutes
- Total abdominal hysterectomy; including laparoscopic assisted
- Vascular surgery (not intra-abdominal)
- Major joint replacement
- Major trauma e.g. lower limb fractures
- Surgery lasting >30 minutes

If none

If present

Is the patient at highest risk of developing VTE?

Anti-embolic stockings (GECS)

Consider intermittent pneumatic compression (IPC)

Consider alternative therapies i.e. warfarin, anti-platelet

YES | NO

HIGHEST RISK
High dose LMWH s/c daily at 1800 hours

MODERATE RISK
Low dose LMWH s/c daily at 1800 hours

C. Emergency patients

Patients admitted, who are eligible for prophylaxis and who are expected to be operated on within 12 hours, should be treated as elective patients admitted on the day of surgery. Naturally, full blood work-up will need to be achieved ASAP as if on-call.

Patients who are admitted after 0900 hours but who are not expected to be operated on until the following day should receive the recommended dose at 1800 hours on the evening of admission.

In all cases

For the purposes of these notes, for surgical patients it is recommended that:

- LMWH prophylaxis should be continued at the same times daily until discharge or until the risk of thromboembolism is considered minimal (the latter most unlikely).

However,

- Consideration should be given to extending prophylaxis when the hospital stay is prolonged or the risk continues. Such prophylaxis is likely to be with warfarin. An alternative is for out-patient treatment or the patient to self-dose with LMWH.

- Continued use of GECS on discharge from hospital to reduce the risk of late VTE may be beneficial in patients with poor mobility.

- NICE recommends that LMWH or fondaparinux therapy should be continued for 4 weeks after hip fracture surgery.

D. Regional Anaesthesia

A major caution is that when epidural/spinal anaesthesia or spinal puncture is employed, patients anticoagulated or scheduled to be anticoagulated with heparin for the prevention of VTE are at risk of developing an epidural or spinal haematoma, which can result in long-term neurological dysfunction.

It is recommended that if LMWH has been administered pre-operatively, a period of 12 hours should elapse – but this may vary with different Trust Guidelines.

Whenever possible, elective surgical admissions should be identified for spinal anaesthesia at the pre-assessment clinic and admitted the day before surgery.

They should then receive a high dose of LMWH at 1800 hours. This will achieve effective prophylaxis combined with minimal additional risk of bleeding complications at the time of regional anaesthesia (e.g. epidural or spinal) and surgery.

In all other cases where the patient has been identified to receive regional anaesthesia, the pre-operative dose of prophylaxis should be withheld, Chemoprophylaxis should then start post-operatively. LMWH should be given no sooner than 4 hours after neural block.

For elective surgical admissions who have attended for pre-assessment, the maintenance dose of LMWH should already have been prescribed for 1800hrs. Therefore, the anaesthetist must give a written instruction not to administer the LMWH dose at 1800 hours if contraindicated.

4: Obstetric surgery (in cases of Caesarean section)

Elective Caesarean sections admitted the night before surgery (see Flowchart 6.3)

In the case of planned Caesarean sections that are admitted the night before, low dose LMWH should be started at 1800 hours the evening before surgery, or if the woman is considered to be at high risk, a high dose of LMWH should be considered following discussion with the consultant responsible for her care. Thereafter, a dose of LMWH (dose dependent on risk) at 1800 hours should be prescribed. Where epidural or spinal anaesthetic has been administered the post-op day dose should be given no sooner than 4 hours after spinal/epidural puncture.

Elective Caesarean sections admitted on the day of surgery (see Flowchart 6.4)

Administer low dose LMWH post-operatively on the day of surgery, provided that this is not within 4 hours if spinal or epidural anaesthesia has been administered. Thereafter, low dose LMWH daily at 1800 hours commencing the next day.

For the purposes of this guideline, for surgical patients it is recommended that:

● Heparin prophylaxis should be continued at the same times daily until discharge or until the risk of thromboembolism is considered minimal.

- Consideration should be given to extending prophylaxis when the hospital stay is prolonged or the risk continues. Such prophylaxis is likely to be with warfarin.
- Continued use of GECS on discharge from hospital to reduce the risk of late VTE may be beneficial in patients with poor mobility.

Flowchart 6.3 Guidelines for Caesarean Section

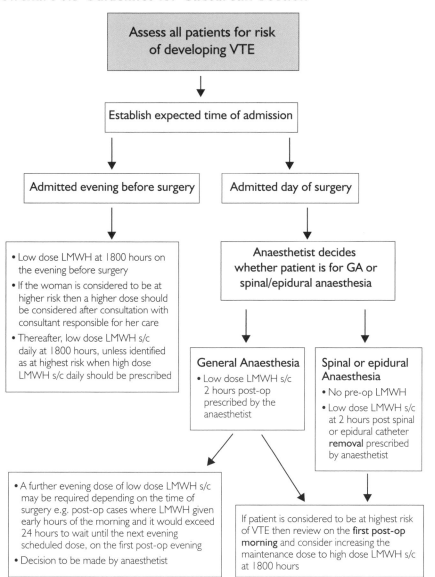

Oral contraceptives and hormone replacement therapy (HRT)

As we have discussed, by themselves, the oral contraceptive pill and HRT are risk factors for VTE, as is surgery. It follows that women taking these synthetic hormones may be at additional risk of VTE should they continue this therapy during surgery. Certainly, such women on HRT undergoing surgery must be assessed for their risk of thrombosis, but there is no evidence in favour of routinely stopping HRT so long as there is appropriate thromboprophylaxis with LMWH or UFH.

Similarly, there is no evidence that the progesterone-only pill is associated with increased risk of VTE, or that such preparations should be stopped prior to surgery. However, whether or not to stop the combined (oestrogen plus progesterone) pill before major surgery is a controversial issue. The risk of unwanted pregnancy, the effects of anaesthesia on pregnancy and the risks of subsequent termination are high, and therefore, rather than stopping the OCP these women should receive thromboprophylaxis with LMWH as per standard guidelines.

Consolidation *(see pages 93–96 for answers)*

6.1 Which 'medical' patients may be in need of anticoagulation?

6.2 Which patient group should be given aspirin?

6.3 What is the most common time of day to give the patient their LMWH?

6.4 What is the role of the anaesthetist in providing anticoagulant cover?

Case Study 3 *For answers see pages 96–98*

A woman who is 14-weeks pregnant, with a history of VTE (previous VTE at 38 weeks of pregnancy) and known to be heterozygous for FVL self-doses with 20 mg of a LMWH daily. At routine screening, her anti-Factor Xa level is 0.5 units/mL (preferred therapeutic range is 0.5–1.0, target prophylactic range is 0.1–0.3 units/mL).

Do you take any action?

Chapter 7

Use of warfarin

General considerations

The National Patient Safety Agency (NPSA) alert 18 (2007)

The document published by the NPSA refers predominantly to anti-thrombotic therapy as is most frequently delivered by warfarin, although use of heparin is briefly addressed. In addition, its prescriptions are demanding as action steps are strongly emphasised. These are:

1. Ensure all staff caring for patients on anticoagulation therapy have the necessary work competences. Any gaps in competence must be addressed through training to ensure that all staff may undertake their duties safely.

2. Review, and, where necessary, update written procedures and clinical protocols to ensure they reflect safe practice, and that staff are trained in these procedures.

3. Audit anticoagulant services using BSH (British Society for Haematology)/NPSA safety indicators as part of the annual medicines management audit programme. The audit results should inform local actions to improve the safe use of anticoagulants, and should be communicated to clinical governance, and drugs and therapeutics committees (or equivalents).

4. Ensure that patients prescribed anticoagulants receive appropriate verbal and written information at the start of therapy, at hospital discharge, on the first anticoagulant clinic appointment, and when necessary throughout the course of their treatment.

5. Promote safe practice with prescribers and pharmacists to check their patients' blood clotting (INR) is being monitored regularly and that the INR level is safe before issuing or dispensing repeat prescriptions for oral anticoagulants.

6. Promote safe practice for prescribers co-prescribing one or more clinically significant interacting medicines for patients already on oral anticoagulants; to make arrangements for additional INR blood tests, and to inform the anti-coagulant service that an interacting medicine has been prescribed.

7. Ensure that dental practitioners manage patients on anticoagulants according to evidence-based therapeutic guidelines. In most cases, dental treatment should proceed as normal and oral anticoagulant treatment should not be stopped or the dosage decreased inappropriately.

8. Amend local policies to standardise the range of anticoagulant products used, incorporating characteristics identified by patients as promoting safer use.

9. Promote the use of written safe practice procedures for the administration of anticoagulants in social care settings. It is safe practice for all dose changes to be confirmed in writing by the prescriber. A risk assessment should be undertaken on the use of Monitored Dosing Systems for anticoagulants for individual patients. The general use of Monitored Dosage Systems for anti-coagulants should be minimised as dosage changes using these systems are more difficult.

> **Key reference**
> www.npsa.nhs.uk/health/alerts

The NPSA documents place considerable responsibility on Trust Thrombosis Teams and Committees to provide training for staff, education for patients, and guidelines for practitioners.

General note

These notes (and indeed, the entire book!) refer to *adult* patients on warfarin. In applying the general principles and recommendations within these notes, the health care professional will need to continue to apply medical and surgical knowledge and clinical judgement to the management of individual patients. These views may not be appropriate in all circumstances. Decisions to adopt any particular actions must be made by the practitioner in the light of available clinical and published resources.

Review of pathophysiology

Recall that warfarin is in fact a slow-acting specific liver poison and as such attention must be paid to adequate liver function (therefore need for LFTs). This is pertinent as this organ is also the site of production of many coagulation proteins. In practice this means that the full effect of a fixed dose of warfarin will not be evident for several days, possibly a week or more. Conversely, the liver will be slow to recover once the drug has been withdrawn. However, vitamin K can be given to promote the return of coagulation protein synthesis.

Warfarin is available in 0.5 mg, 1 mg, 3 mg and 5 mg tablets. Patients take a combination daily with an aim to maintain an INR either between 2 and 3 (hence target 2.5), or between 3 and 4 (hence target 3.5). In practice the average dose is 4–6 mg daily. The INR is monitored with venous blood or by fingerprick. Management is by simple up- or down-titration followed by re-testing. In case of low INR (at either target), the patient is advised to increase their daily dose of warfarin, and vice versa for an INR above the desired range. Precise algorithms for these dose changes and return visits for rechecking are provided below.

Management

Patients may be classified as follows:

1. Patients presenting to hospital (e.g. for surgery) whilst already on warfarin

2. Patients who have to be started on warfarin whilst an in-patient (e.g. following orthopaedic surgery). Consider the patient's suitability for warfarin treatment if new to warfarin (see Table 5.4).

I. The patient being admitted is already on warfarin

Therefore, by definition, the patient is already at risk of thrombosis. It is likely that the purpose of the hospital visit will increase this risk, and in almost all cases use of LMWH will be advised. The difficulty is therefore the extent to which warfarin must be reduced and re-introduced after the particular procedure that demanded in-patient attendance.

It is very likely that the patient's INR will change in accordance with hospital admission (i.e. effects of diet, mobility, other treatments) and in consequence the INR will need to be checked at least every 48 hours, possibly every 24 hours. Common reasons for patients to be presenting are for surgery and for cardioversion of atrial fibrillation back to normal rhythm.

The patient is admitted for surgery

Here, the risk of VTE from stopping warfarin needs to be balanced against the risks of bleeding during surgery. The following should be addressed:

- The option to stop warfarin therapy preoperatively and perform the procedure when the INR has returned to safe levels; administer full-dose anticoagulation with LMWH; or administer prophylactic doses of LMWH.

- The individual's risk of bleeding will vary both with the type of surgery, and with the presence of other risk factors for bleeding. Most surgery can be safely performed when the INR falls to 1.5.

- Period of time for INR to fall: for patients in a therapeutic range of INR 2–3, it takes approximately 4 days after stopping warfarin for INR to reach 1.5; for patients with a therapeutic range INR 3–4 and the elderly this may be longer.

The patient is admitted for elective surgery

Minor risk of VTE

- For minor surgery an INR of < 2 should be achieved. For very minor procedures: some surgeons may operate at INR 2.5.
- For an INR range 2–3: omit warfarin for 2 days.
- INR range 3–4: omit warfarin for 3–4 days.
- Restart warfarin post-operatively on the day of surgery at the maintenance dose (occasionally a boost in the dose of Warfarin will be required).

Medium risk of VTE

These will be patients on long-term anticoagulants for atrial fibrillation, cardiomyopathy, previous single episode of VTE more than three months ago, mural thrombus, rheumatic mitral valve disease, new model prosthetic aortic valves, tissue valves.

Before surgery:
- Stop warfarin 4 days prior to surgery. If INR still high a small dose of vitamin K (0.5–1 mg orally) may be given if necessary.
- Consider stopping anti-platelet drugs (aspirin, clopidogrel) 5–7 days before surgery.
- Give high dose LMWH at 1800 hours or at least 12 hours before operation.
- On the morning of surgery check that the INR is < 1.5

After surgery:
- Continue high dose LMWH daily post-operatively as above.
- Restart warfarin as soon as patient is able to take oral fluids.
- When INR > 2 for 48 hours stop LMWH.

High risk of VTE

Patients on long-term anticoagulants for prosthetic mitral valve, old model aortic prosthetic valves, recurrent VTE, antiphospholipid syndrome, recent (within 3 months) VTE. Patients who have had VTE (especially PE within the last month) are considered very high risk. If surgery is urgent and there are risk factors for bleeding, IVC filters should be considered.

Before surgery:
- Recall that the risk of haemorrhage is greater than the risk of recurrent VTE, providing sub-therapeutic INRs are limited to 1–2 days only.
- Generally, stop warfarin 4–5 days before surgery, consider stopping anti-platelets 5–7 days before surgery.
- Admit 2 days prior to surgery, check INR on admission and daily. In some cases low dose LMWH can be used when the INR is < 2.0, with a prophylactic dose given the night prior to surgery.
- The interval between full dose LMWH and surgery should be 24 hours; and 12 hours between prophylactic LMWH and surgery.

Day of surgery:
- Check INR and APTT.
- If INR < 1.8, proceed with operation, if > 1.8; delay operation.
- A small dose of vitamin K, e.g. 0.5–1 mg IV will lower the INR. The onset of action of IV vitamin K is 6–8 hours and it may take 3 to 4 days for warfarin to work when re-started.
- LMWH will need to be continued post-op.

After surgery;

- Restart therapeutic low dose of LMWH 12 hours post-op. Monitoring should not be necessary, but if so this can be achieved with anti-Xa levels.
- Restart warfarin at the usual dose on the evening of the operation or as soon as the patient is able to take oral fluids and provided there is no undue bleeding.
- Continue LMWH and warfarin until INR > 2.5 (this is usually 5–7 days).
- Monitor INR daily – however, be cautious in increasing the dose of warfarin too rapidly, recalling that warfarin is a slow acting poison.
- For patients who are at a higher risk of bleeding IV unfractionated heparin is preferable as it has a shorter duration of action than warfarin or LMWH, and is more rapidly reversible although monitoring by APTT is required.

The patient is admitted for emergency surgery

- Again consider if minor or major surgery – does the INR need to be lowered? (See above).
  - If INR is > 2.0 and urgent reversal is required, stop anti-coagulant therapy, take blood samples (INR, FBC, crossmatch, other tests if indicated).
  - If there is sufficient time before surgery, give vitamin K 0.5 mg IV slowly. This will lower the INR in roughly 6–8 hours. The patient may be refractory to warfarin for 3–4 days after but this can be covered with LMWH.
  - Larger doses of IV vitamin K 5–10 mg can be given if continued anti-coagulation is not needed again.
  - Check INR prior to surgery: if > 2.0 and surgery is urgent and there is no time for vitamin K to work, give FFP 10–15 mls/kg or prothrombin complex concentrates.
  - Repeat INR after FFP and before surgery: When INR < 2.0, proceed with operation.
- Note that separate actions exist for management of in-patients who are over-anticoagulated (Table 8.2). Restart warfarin in the post-op period as above with regard to risks of thrombosis/haemorrhage. Ensure the patient is fully educated as to the purpose of therapy.

The patient is admitted for cardioversion for atrial fibrillation (AF)

It is already established that AF is a risk factor for thrombotic stroke and therefore requires thromboprophylaxis, almost exclusively with warfarin (INR range 2–3).

This should be indefinite (i.e. for life) as the chances of the heartbeat returning to (normal) sinus rhythm are remote in nature and thus the risk of stroke will be present for life. However, pharmacotherapy may be effective, but if this fails or is inappropriate, there is cardioversion. This is effectively an attempt to shock the heart back to sinus rhythm with electricity. Unfortunately this procedure in itself can precipitate a stroke. This may be because of the effect of the cardioversion, although it may also result from the embolism of an existing intra-cardiac thrombus. In either case, the risk of this cardioversion-precipitated stroke can be reduced by anticoagulation.

A common regime is to ensure INR range 2–3 for several weeks both before and after cardioversion. Almost by definition, the patient will be on warfarin for weeks if not months before cardioversion, hence in practice it will simply be a matter of withdrawing the warfarin once sinus rhythm has been re-established (as proven by electrocardiogram).

2. The patient being admitted needs to be started on warfarin

Introduction

Local guidelines should be developed by a thrombosis committee to ensure a safe, effective and consistent approach to the management of adult patients in primary and secondary care receiving warfarin. Often, the prescribing information contained in published guidelines is issued on the understanding that it is the best practice from available resources at the time of issue. The latest recommendations from the British Committee for Standards in Haematology should be followed. Teams should also be aware of the latest NPSA patient safety alert already mentioned.

Each Trust's/PCT's documents must give advice to prescribers and other healthcare professionals on managing patients on warfarin, e.g. prescribing considerations, monitoring requirements and factors affecting warfarin therapy. The user is reminded of the importance of the patient's handheld record in the form of an anticoagulant therapy record booklet. Due to the inherent complexity associated with warfarin use, communication between teams involved in patient care is of utmost importance particularly since very often patients are initiated in secondary care and managed in primary care.

Key points

- Ensure the patient is actually able to take warfarin (Table 5.4)

- Establish diagnosis, target INR and duration of therapy

- Assess patient compliance; identify any problems which may indicate patient will not comply with treatment and monitoring

- Baseline investigations: LFTs, FBC, APTT/PT, U&Es, creatinine

- Full medical history and medication history at start, then regularly

- Anticoagulant therapy record booklet supplied, completed, and patient taken through information systematically

- Ensure adequate communication between primary and secondary care.

Q: Who should be treated with warfarin ?

A: Those in whom the benefits of warfarin outweigh the possible disadvantages.

Likely candidates for the prescription include those at risk of thrombosis (e.g. following orthopaedic surgery), but also those with a history of existing thrombosis (i.e. previous or current PE and/or DVT).

Q. How long should treatment last ?

A. As long as the risk factor remains active.

So for risk factors such as surgery or childbirth, treatment will not be for long. If the risk factor is cancer – this may be until cured. Patients with recurrent VTEs (i.e. are thrombophilic) will also be long-term users. (See Table 5.1.)

Table 7.1 Target INRs and recommended duration of anticoagulation

Indication	INR target	Duration
Pulmonary Embolus	2.5	6 months
Distal DVT due to temporary risk factors	2.5	3 months
Proximal DVT or DVT of unknown cause or those associated with ongoing risk factors	2.5	6 months
VTE associated with malignancy	2.5	6 months then review
Recurrence of VTE – NOT on warfarin	2.5	Long term
Recurrence of VTE – WHILST on warfarin	3.5	Long term
Atrial fibrillation	2.5	Long term
AF for cardioversion (CV)	2.75	4 weeks pre-CV min. 4 weeks post
Cardiomyopathy	2.5	Long term
Mural thrombus	2.5	3 months
Rheumatic mitral valve disease	2.5	Long term
Mechanical prosthetic heart valves (Aortic)*	3.0	Long term
Mechanical prosthetic heart valves (Mitral)*	3.5	Long term
Antiphospholipid syndrome (VTE)	2.5	Long term
Antiphospholipid syndrome (arterial thrombosis)	3.5	Long term
Thrombophilias	Discuss with haematologist	

*according to BCSH guidelines target INRs may vary depending on valve type, if unsure use generic target for valve location. Patients referred to the anticoagulant clinic will be assigned a target INR as per BCSH guidelines UNLESS reasonable evidence is given to the contrary.

Induction of warfarin

SAFETY: As with heparins, not all patients will be able to take warfarin and all must be assessed (Table 5.4). The clinical, cognitive and social status of the patient should be assessed to ensure they are willing and able to take the drug as intended and attend for regular blood tests. Anticoagulation is contraindicated in a number of situations where the risks of harm are likely to outweigh the benefits of treatment. Many contraindications are relative rather than absolute.

General considerations

There are two approaches to the induction of anticoagulation: slow or rapid. Slow induction can be initiated in out-patient anticoagulant clinics but may be considered in patients for imminent discharge. Referrals may be considered for rapid induction in the community. Patients will not be started on warfarin without:

- A comprehensive diagnosis (i.e. not simply 'DVT – please treat', but, for example, 'DVT secondary to prostatic cancer – please treat'). The desired target INR (generally 2.5 or 3.5 – if not, justify).

- The duration of treatment (3 months, 6 months, long term).

For all patients:

- Take baseline blood samples (LFTs, FBC, APTT/PT, U&Es, creatinine), full medical history (any cautions or contraindications, pregnancy) and full medication history (consider interactions, herbal and over the counter medicines).

- Each Trust should have its own set of guidelines, and this must include a dedicated form for patient information.

- Give patients/carers verbal and written information regarding their treatment, complete patient education checklist and insert in patients' records. The NPSA patient information packs are available from pharmacy and are available in different languages.

Rapid induction

This is generally for patients at high and/or acute risk of VTE, and will be the dominant procedure for in-patients. Rapid anticoagulation should achieve the target INR within 5 days. Heparin and warfarin should be started together and heparin continued until the INR has been within range for two consecutive days. Subcutaneous heparin is usually the treatment of choice for VTE and acute coronary syndromes.

Where rapid induction of warfarin is required follow the normogram (e.g. Table 7.2). Care should be taken for patients with a low body weight (less than 50 kg), elderly patients, those with a low albumin, liver or heart disease, or multiple interacting medications. In such cases a lower loading dose, e.g. 5mg on day 1 should be used. In some cases slow induction should be considered.

> **REMEMBER:** Warfarin requirements can vary immediately post-op and with heart and liver disease and in elderly patients – suggest use smaller loading. Beware drug interactions and polypharmacy: *See BNF before prescribing new treatment.*

Patients who have recently commenced oral anticoagulant therapy as in-patients will need their INR checking regularly, usually by venepuncture on alternate days within the first week. Once stabilised, time between INR checks can lengthen but changes in interacting medications must be accompanied by more frequent checks. As discussed, patients (especially undergoing surgery) may be started on LMWH and warfarin at the same time. However, this may be altered by the use of LMWH, especially for those who are self-dosing.

Table 7.2 Daily dose of warfarin to achieve rapid induction of INR 2–3

INR day I (before Rx)	Warfarin dose	INR day 2	Warfarin dose	INR day 3	Warfarin dose	INR day 4	Warfarin dose on day 4 and maintenance dose
< 1.4	10 mg	< 1.4	10 mg	< 1.4	12 mg	< 1.4	15 mg
		1.4–1.7	6 mg	1.4–2.1	5 mg	1.4	8 mg
		1.8–3.8	1 mg	2.2–2.5	4 mg	1.5–1.7	7 mg
		> 3.9	none	2.6–2.9	3 mg	1.8–1.9	6 mg
				3.0–3.3	2 mg	2.0–2.4	5 mg
				3.4–3.5	1 mg	2.5–3.2	4 mg
				3.6–4.0	0.5 mg	3.3–4.0	3 mg
				> 4.5	None	4.1–4.5	Miss next dose then 2 mg
						> 4.5	Miss two doses then 1 mg

NOTE: baseline INRs > 1.4 discuss with haematology consultant. For INRs > 5 see the section on over-anticoagulation (Tables 8.1, 8.2).

Slow induction

It follows that this route will be applicable (mostly) to out-patients.

Many patients diagnosed with AF are deemed to be of relatively low VTE risk (daily TIA/CVA rate no higher than 1/1000 per day). As the vast majority are from an ageing population, rapid introduction is neither warranted nor safe. In the latter regard, both advanced age and recent initiation are risk factors for major warfarin-related haemorrhage.

It must be borne in mind that many of these patients may already be on a number of other medications, including those with known potential for interaction with anticoagulants. This patient group may also have hepatic congestion arising out of congestive cardiac failure, with further pharmacodynamic implications. Some patients are also likely to have reduced renal function. Finally, it is important to establish from the patient's GP/secondary care physician (often, but not always, a cardiologist) whether the patient should remain on anti-platelet therapy, e.g. aspirin/clopidogrel alongside oral anticoagulation.

The induction regimen of choice is determined by the baseline capillary INR and the presence or absence of various risk factors, e.g. age ≥70 years, CCF, relevant previous bleeding history (e.g. haematuria), polypharmacy (especially if ≥3 potential interactions), excessive alcohol intake, coexistent aspirin/clopidogrel, social isolation etc. (there could be others in individual cases). Table 7.3 gives a typical scheme.

Table 7.3 Daily dose of warfarin to achieve slow induction of INR 2–3 (e.g. as out-patient)

Baseline INR	Risk Factors	Daily warfarin dose	Repeat INR
< 1– 1. 2	No	4 mg	1 week
1.3–1.4	No	3.5 mg	1 week
< 1– 1. 2	Yes	3 mg	1 week
1.3–1.4	Yes	2.5 mg	3 days

Subsequent dosing

Increase 0.5 mg to 1 mg daily until INR 2–3, return in 3–7 days depending on INR. If INR > 3, then reduce dose accordingly. If baseline INR is > 1.4 – discuss with consultant haematologist. Further investigations may need to be undertaken prior to this patient receiving warfarin as an outpatient. For INR 3–4, adopt similar method but 1 mg/day higher.

Re-starting patients' warfarin therapy.

Patients who have stopped warfarin therapy (for example, due to surgery) will need re-inducting on warfarin depending on their reasons for anticoagulation. Usually, patients with simple AF may just need to restart their warfarin on their usual dose (taking into consideration any changes in medication or general well being). The risks of over anticoagulation and bleeding associated with rapid induction should be considered. Patients with prosthetic valves may need anticoagulation cover with heparin until INR is within range depending on the age and valve type. Patients with a history of or recent VTE should receive heparin until INR is back within range. In both cases warfarin should be inducted rapidly. Consideration needs to be given post-operatively to increased risks of bleeding.

The Yellow Book

In the UK perhaps 500,000 people are taking warfarin. A handy, if not invaluable, record of their treatment dose and INR is in the form of a Yellow Book that will be issued to each patient when they start on warfarin. It contains not only a record of the patients' warfarin use, but also helpful tips as to how the patients can help themselves, and what possible problems to be aware of. Patients are encouraged to take care of this book and bring it with them each time they attend hospital or their GP.

Generally:

● Patients induced as in-patients will inevitably convert to out-patients

● Some out-patients with special needs (e.g. poor mobility) may need to be treated at home, i.e. are 'domiciliary' patients

● Many out-patients will be ultimately transferred to outreach clinics, generally in GP surgeries, health care centres etc.

Consolidation

(see pages 93–96 for answers)

7.1 What government agency has published a major document on the general management of warfarin?

7.2 Why should patients about to undergo surgery be taken off warfarin and what is the alternative anticoagulant?

7.3 How long should treatment with warfarin last?

7.4 What kinds of patients require rapid induction or slow induction of warfarin?

On-going management of warfarin

All major teaching hospitals and DGHs have an Oral Anticoagulant Therapy (OAT) Clinic, set up to serve possibly hundreds of patients taking (mostly) warfarin, although there is an alternative for those intolerant of this drug (phenindione). As discussed, warfarin is the most effective agent for reducing the risk of thrombosis, e.g. of thrombotic stroke in AF, and of a recurrent VTE, out-performing aspirin.

However, poor pharmacokinetics means it must be monitored frequently with a blood test (generally a thumb prick). Most hospitals provide this monitoring service for consultant colleagues or GPs, but once the INR has been checked it is logistically sensible to offer advice on management at the same time (i.e. on increasing or decreasing the daily dose of warfarin to be taken).

The objective of treatment with warfarin is to provide maximum reduction in risk of thrombosis with minimum risk of haemorrhage. For most patients, this is INR range 2–3. INR < 1.6 (for example) provides low risk of haemorrhage but poor reduction in the risk of thrombosis. Similarly, a patient with INR 4.5 has superb protection against a thrombus but a high risk of bleeding.

Almost all literature deals with inappropriately high levels of INR, and mostly ignores a sub-therapeutic INR. However, many consider patients with a recent VTE to be at increased risk of recurrence, so that those with a sub-therapeutic INR of, shall we say, 1.2, on two concurrent visits, may need urgent LMWH (perhaps 20 mg or 40 mg) to minimise the risk of thrombosis until the INR is in its target range of 2–3.

Up- or down-titrate

At the practical level, a patient with an INR above target will be advised to cut down their daily dose, whilst those with an INR below range will be advised to increase their dose (i.e. up- or down-titration). Both sets of patients are then advised to return at an interval of 1–3 weeks (depending on history, risk factor profile, how far they are out of ideal target range).

Warfarin is offered in 0.5, 1, 3 and 5 mg tablets, and the daily dose is made up by a combination. Cutting tablets in half is discouraged, so for 4.5 mg a day, a patient will be instructed to take 4 mg or 5 mg on alternate days. But if, say, 4.5 mg is too much, and 4mg too little, then 4.25 mg seems correct. However, a daily or alternative day regime for this is impossible, but in practice, it may be achieved by taking 4 mg each day, but 5 mg on Wednesdays and Sundays, so that over the week it smoothes out. Conversely, for a desired average dose of 3.75 mg daily (where 4 mg a day is too much but 3 mg/4 mg alternate days is not enough), a weekly regime would be 4 mg a day but only 3 mg on Wednesday and Sunday.

In two published studies the typical daily dose of warfarin used by *low-risk* out-patients (i.e. INR target 2.5) was 4.5 mg/day. Similarly, the typical daily dose used by *high-risk* out-patients (i.e. INR target 3.5) was 5.75 mg/day (Blann and Bareford, 2001 and Blann *et al.*, 1999).

Problems with management

Regrettably, as mentioned, the efficacy of warfarin is influenced by many factors that frustrate the objective of perfect INR control (Table 7.4). In practice, this means there is a considerable variability in its effect on patients, and its effectiveness is often influenced by factors such as age, racial background, diet and the use of other medications such as antibiotics. This will be revisited in due course.

Table 7.4 Patient factors that influence the efficacy of warfarin

Enhanced Anticoagulant Effect	Reduced Anticoagulant Effect
Excess alcohol ingestion	Weight gain
Increased age (e.g. > 80 years)	Diarrhoea & vomiting
Heart and renal failure	Relative youth (e.g. age < 40 years)
Impaired liver function	Non white European background

Management options

A common model operates in two out-patient department rooms with a health care assistant, an occasional clerical assistant, a scientist, and a dosing officer (DO), all managed by a senior biomedical scientist with two full time clerical assistants, and is heavily dependent on software. It caters for around 100 patients three times a week who attend at regular intervals throughout a morning (9.30 to 12.30 pm) or afternoon (1.30 to 4.30 p.m.) session.

1. Upon arrival, ideally at the rate of three per five minutes, patients are 'booked in' by a health care assistant and queue up to have their blood checked. A

clerical assistant is present for the first hour or so to sort out any administrative problems, such as lost details or new patients.

2. In one room, capillary blood is obtained by thumb prick and the INR is derived by a biomedical scientist on a small coagulation machine that is dedicated for this purpose. The scientist writes the INR result in the Yellow Book.

3. *Option 1:* If the INR is *within* range (e.g. 2.2 in the range 2–3) the patient is verbally recommended to continue taking the same daily dose. The Yellow Book is retained and the patient is told he/she will receive it in the post, and then sent home. The Yellow Book is than passed to a second room where the dosing officer (DO, perhaps a scientist or pharmacist) will write in his/her recommen-dation and enter the details on a computer. The computer then offers a future appointment (up to a maximum of 12 weeks) that the DO writes in the Yellow Book. At the end of the clinic all retained Yellow Books are posted out 1st class to the patients by a clerical assistant.

4. *Option 2:* If the INR is *out of* range (e.g. 1.3 or 3.6 in the range 2–3) the patient (taking their Yellow Book with them) is invited to consult in the adjoining room with the DO, to discuss the abnormal result, who invites suggestions for causes (e.g. missed doses, use of antibiotics, change of dose of another drug). The DO then decides/negotiates appropriate action (i.e. increase/decrease daily dose) and, with the help of the computer, offers the patient a future appointment to re-test their INR. The patient then leaves, taking their Yellow Book with them.

Training

The NPSA safety alert emphasises that all staff interacting with anticoagulant control of patients *will* be appropriately trained. This is likely to be organised by the Thrombosis Committee and delivered by a senior biomedical scientist.

Other models

In another model patients are venesected from an ante-cubital vein in out-patients, or in a side room of the laboratory. The patients then wait as their blood passes (via porter or pneumatic chute) to the laboratory for INR generation which is telephoned back to clinic. The DO then consults directly with the patient and notes are made in the Yellow book. Patients may be offered a targeted appointment (e.g. 10.15 a.m.) or are invited to attend at any time within the three hours of a session. This model therefore saves some effort in out-patient clinics but places more stress on the phlebotomy service and the main laboratory.

Beyond the hospital

The safety and efficacy of oral-anticoagulant therapy (essentially, warfarin) is such that it can be transferred from the hospital to general practice. Several models exist:

A: Patients are venesected at their practice, generally by the practice nurse, who retains the Yellow Book. The blood tube passes to the local DGH laboratory (van, post) where the INR is generated. Results are passed back to the GP (telephone, fax, email) for him/her to manage with the patient (via the Yellow Book) as appropriate.

B: As above, but the Yellow Book also passed to the hospital where the INR is generated. The DO later contacts the patient directly (at home/mobile) with recommendations to remain on the same dose or change to a different daily dose as appropriate, and return as necessary. The Yellow Book is returned to the patient in the post.

C: The local DGH provides the scientific personnel and equipment into the practice to generate an INR immediately from the patient, probably by thumb prick. The results and Yellow Book are then taken back to the hospital for computer-assisted dosing, and patients are then managed from the hospital as (B) above.

D: As C, but patient's result is immediately translated into a recommendation by a local DO provided by the hospital who is equipped with a laptop loaded with the dosing software. The DO then consults immediately with the patients. This then is essentially an entire hospital out-patient clinic transferred to the practice.

E: The practice runs their own clinic with a Near-Patient-Testing (NPT) device completely independent of the hospital.

Naturally there are logistical and economic implications of each model for the hospital finance officers and the practice managers to consider.

Consolidation

(see pages 93–96 for answers)

7.5 What is the general method for changing a patient's warfarin dose to ensure their INR is in range?

7.6 What is the approximate average daily dose of warfarin taken by low-risk patients?

7.7 What is the approximate average daily dose of warfarin taken by high-risk patients?

7.8 What patient factors influence the dose of warfarin?

Case Study 4 *For answers see pages 96–98*

A 71-year-old man with hypertension and diabetes has been found to have AF. He is started on a loading dose of warfarin 10 mg on day 1, 5 mg on days 2 and 3, and then 4 mg daily by the anticoagulant team. His first and serial visits to the OAT Clinic are as follows

Date	INR	Recommended daily dose of warfarin	Next visit (weeks)
5th October	1.5	4 mg/5 mg alternate days	1
12th October	1.9	Same dose	1
19th October	2.4	Same dose	2
2nd November	1.8	Same dose	1
9th November	1.5	5 mg daily	1
16th November	2.7	Same dose	2
30th November	2.9	Same dose	3
21st December	3.7		

What are your questions and what is your recommendation?

Case Study 5 *For answers see pages 96–98*

In the 24th September Warfarin Clinic, an 80-year-old woman with a long-standing artificial mechanical heart valve and a history of cardiovascular disease is sent in to see the dosing officer with her Yellow Book. It has the following history:

Date	INR	Recommended daily dose of warfarin	Next visit (weeks)
4th May	3.8	3 mg/4 mg alternate days	3
25th May	3.2	Same dose	4
22nd June	3.9	Same dose	3
13th August	4.1	Same dose	3
3rd September	3.8	Same dose	4
24th September	4.3		

What are your questions and what is your recommendation?

Chapter 8

What happens if something goes wrong?
– Haemorrhage

How big a problem is this? According to the National Patient Safety Agency, there were 480 reported cases of harm or near harm from the use of anticoagulants in the UK from 1990–2002. In addition, there have been 120 deaths reported over the same time period. Deaths from the use of warfarin were responsible for 77% (92 people) and heparin for 23% (28 people) of reports.

Heparin

Because unfractionated heparin and LMWHs have a short half-life, problems can often resolve quite rapidly by simply stopping the treatment. However, serious haemorrhage (definition – as for warfarin) is treated by protamine sulphate (non-proprietary or Prosulf: see the BNF) given by slow IV infusion. Generally, 1 mg neutralises 80–100 units of heparin. The maximum dose is 50 mg as an excess can have an anticoagulant effect. Curiously, cautions include fish allergy, men who are infertile or who have had a vasectomy. An alternative to protamine sulphate is infusion of fresh frozen plasma or Factor VII. However, the problems are almost always ward-based and due to unfractionated heparin.

Warfarin

An increasing INR brings a risk of haemorrhage that demands action as it may be fatal or at least seriously debilitating (e.g. haemorrhagic stroke). A major problem is that as warfarin has a long half-life, changes are slow and so will not be evident in less than a few days. But what is haemorrhage? Examples include bloodshot eyes, blood in the mouth after brushing teeth, bleeding after shaving, bruising over arms/legs etc. How seriously should this be taken?

Certainly, vomiting and urinating blood are serious and demand attention. But how much blood has been lost? An obvious answer is to look for a reduction in the haemoglobin level of the full blood count. Generally, a two-unit fall is considered serious and may demand a blood transfusion. This, of course, demands a recent FBC. In the case of an effective overdose of warfarin options are to reduce or stop the drug and give the antidote, vitamin K. Table 8.1 is an example of a regime for managing a high INR as an out-patient.

IMPORTANT

This scheme is based on practice but is NOT to be taken as usable in your setting.

Your local OAT clinic will have their own scheme written by the Thrombosis Committee and based on firm British Society for Haematology Guidelines.

High INR in an out-patient (Table 8.1)

Therapeutic decisions are dependent on the INR, whether there is minor or major bleeding, other risk factors for bleeding (e.g. age > 70 years, previous bleeding complications) and reason for anticoagulation.

In all cases the patient's current warfarin dose stability, concurrent medications and clinical condition must be considered when advising dose change and date of retest. One or two days of a reduced dose may be worthwhile in some cases before resumption of the new dose. Significant bleeding (e.g. haematuria) with any INR result should be discussed with a haematologist. Anticoagulant services will refer immediately to A&E *(Inform A&E of their imminent arrival)*.

Any out patient receiving oral anticoagulants who may be experiencing a major bleeding episode should be advised to seek urgent medical attention from the nearest A&E department.

High INR in an in-patient (Table 8.2)

Clearly, being an in-patient implies some serious medical or surgical issue. Important factors to know include INR, any current or previous bleeding, reason

Table 8.1 Action in response to a high INR in an out-patient

INR	Potential action
3.1–3.5 (only if target INR 2.5)	Consider same dose (e.g. if 3.1) or reduce by about 5% (e.g. if 3.5). Possibly miss one dose, retest in one/two weeks.
3.6–4.0 (only if target INR 2.5)	Reduce dose by about 5–10%. Possibly miss one dose, retest in 5 days–one week.
4.1–5.9	Consider stopping warfarin for 1 to 2 days. Recommence on reduced dose (about 10–15%). Retest within 2 to 5 days.
6.0–6.9	Stop warfarin for 2 to 3 days. Recommence warfarin on reduced dose (about 15–20%). Retest in 1 to 4 days
7.0–7.9	Stop warfarin for 2 to 3 days. Recommence warfarin on reduced dose (about 20–30%). Retest next day .
8.0–8.9	Stop warfarin. Consider vitamin K oral 1.0 mg, retest next day.
9.0–11.9	Stop warfarin. Consider vitamin K oral 1.0–2.0 mgs, retest next day.
12.0–14.9	Inform consultant haematologist. Give vitamin K, oral, 2 mg. Stop warfarin, retest next day.
15.0–20.0	Inform consultant haematologist. Give vitamin K oral 2.5 – 5.0 mgs. Stop warfarin, retest the next day.

for anticoagulation, patient age/diagnosis (elderly patients are more likely to bleed). Bleeding at therapeutic INR needs investigation for local cause.

Other diagnoses, e.g. cardiac failure (hence need to know left ventricle ejection fraction), liver dysfunction (hence need to request LFTs), renal dysfunction (hence need to request urea, creatinine and electrolytes), are relevant not only in identifying the cause but also in predicting responses to treatment.

Table 8.2 Action in response to a high INR in an in-patient

INR	Potential action
3.1–6.0 (only if target INR 2.5)	Reduce warfarin dose or stop. Restart when INR < 5.0.
4.0–6.0 (only if target INR 3.5)	Reduce warfarin dose or stop. Restart when INR < 5.0.
6.0–8.0 No bleeding or minor bleeding	Stop warfarin, restart when INR < 5.0, consider vitamin K 0.5–1.0 mg orally.
> 8.0 No bleeding or minor bleeding	Stop warfarin, restart when INR < 5.0 if wish to anticoagulate again. If other risk factors for bleeding, give 2.5 mg vitamin K oral or IV (for INRs 12–20 give 5 mg vitamin K). Repeat dose of vitamin K after 24 hours if INR still high. Seek advice.
Major bleeding	Stop warfarin. Give prothrombin complex concentrate (Beriplex) 50 units/Kg or FFP 15 ml/Kg. Give 5mg vitamin K IV Repeat dose of vitamin K after 24 hours if INR still high. Seek advice.

Intravenous vitamin K rarely causes allergy and is generally safe. The IV preparation Konakion MM Paediatric can be given orally. The degree of reversal with vitamin K varies on individual basis, e.g. patients with prosthetic valves may require FFP only and a very small dose of vitamin K to avoid oral anticoagulant resistance later. IV vitamin K reverses more rapidly than oral vitamin K and should be used if reversal is urgent.

Causes of haemorrhage

An attempt must be made to establish the cause of over-anticoagulation in case this impacts upon further treatment. Consideration should be given to the need for the patient to continue on anticoagulation in the presence of contraindications e.g. age, non-compliance. But without doubt the leading cause of haemorrhage is drug interaction, and of these, antibiotics are the main culprits.

Other established risk factors include patient confusion, recent return from holiday, age, binge use of alcohol, and inadequate education leading to poor compliance (especially warfarin). Significant drug interactions are listed in appendix 1 of the BNF. If the patient has bled as a result of the interaction or requires admission to hospital a yellow card should be completed and sent to the MHRA.

Some Drug Interactions with Warfarin

- Analgesics: NSAIDs, celecoxib, ibuprofen, diclofenac, aspirin, paracetamol

- Antibacterials: Neomycin, chloramphenicol, erythromycin

- Antidepressants: Venlafaxine, St John's Wort, tricyclics

- Cytotoxics: Fluorouracil, azathioprine, mercaptopurine

- Lipid-regulators   Colestyramine, rosuvastatin, fibrates, simvastatin

- Ulcer-healers   Cimetidine, esomeprazole, omeprazole, sucralfate

...and, curiously, cranberry juice!

If a drug interaction is suspected and/or can be predicted, it may be necessary to alter the dose of the particular drug and/or that of warfarin. But which way? And which drug is more important? Increased monitoring is likely.

Patient reassurance and education

It is likely that the haemorrhaging patient (whether on warfarin or heparin) will be very concerned and so reassurance is required. In addition, this will provide an opportunity to reinforce patient education with regards to risk factors and concomitant medications.

Consolidation

(see pages 93–96 for answers)

8.1 What is the antidote for excess heparin?

8.2 What are the first actions in cases of excess warfarin?

8.3 What are the treatments for life threatening haemorrhage?

8.4 Which commonly-prescribed drugs interact with warfarin?

Case Study 6 *For answers see pages 96–98*

A 65-year-old man with no English visits the Anticoagulation Clinic with his wife and an interpreter. The indication for warfarin is DVT and his duration of treatment is 6 months. His Yellow Book gives the following history, starting with 6 mg, but 7 mg on Wednesdays and Sundays.

Date (weeks)	INR	Recommended daily dose of warfarin	Next visit (weeks)
8th October	2.5	Same dose	3
22nd October	1.5	Same dose	1
29th October	2.9	Same dose	2
12th November	4.0	Miss one dose, then resume	1
19th November	3.1	Same dose	2

3rd December	1.2	6 mg/7 mg alternate days	1
10th December	2.8	Same dose	2
24th December	8.5	Stop warfarin, 1 mg Vitamin K given	(4 days)
28th December	3.2	5 mg daily	(3 days)
31st December	2.1	6 mg daily	1
7th January	1.5	6 mg/7 mg alternate days	1
14th January	1.3	7 mg daily	1
21st January	3.6		

What to do?...

Case Study 7 *For answers see pages 96–98*

A 56-year-old man comes in to see you in the Oral-Anticoagulant Clinic in a state of extreme anxiety because the sclera (the white part) of his left eye is completely red. You admit it looks bad. He says that he had an irritation in the eye a few days ago and rubbed it hard for several minutes. His INR is 2.4 (target 2.5).

What to do?...

Case Study 8 *For answers see pages 96–98*

A 63-year-old woman comes to the Oral-Anticoagulant Clinic in advance of her appointment. She reports a history of occasional blood in her urine over the past ten days, and has had two nosebleeds. Her INR today is 8.5.

What to do?...

Summary

VTE is far from a benign condition: ten years after thrombosis:

- Over half (56%) will have suffered post-thrombotic syndrome

- 29% will have suffered a recurrent VTE

- 28% will be dead: mostly from cancer, myocardial infarction or stroke.

VTE, comprising DVT and PE, are common and treatable both in hospital and in the community. Established treatments are:

- **Warfarin** is a most effective oral anticoagulant. However, misuse confers a significant risk of bleeding, there is no common dose, it is difficult to control, and is sensitive to numerous commonly-prescribed drugs. Yet despite these drawbacks it remains a powerful agent for the reduction of various VTEs in many different circumstances.

- Developed from unfractionated heparin, **LMWH** is currently becoming the therapy of choice in many conditions where thrombosis is to be avoided or, at least, minimised. However, recent guidelines for the use of unfractionated heparin suggest some value.

- **Fondaparinux** is slowly becoming established and is appearing in guidelines.

Treatment agent(s) and duration (3 months, 6 months, life) depend on the persistence of the cause/risk factor. Major risk factors include increasing age, recent surgery (especially orthopaedic), cancer (especially active) and thrombophilia.

Tips for Practitioners

When faced with a patient with suspected or actual DVT or PE, relevant steps (often in collaboration with secondary care) include:

1. Assess the clinical state of the patient, e.g. symptoms, haemodynamic stability, etc.

2. Assess risk factors for a DVT or PE, and manage the correctable ones.

3. Assess the diagnostic probability of a DVT or PE.

4. If DVT, consider outpatient management or referral to specialist centre. If PE suspected, refer to hospital.

5. Have a clear management plan with regard to treatment (warfarin and/or LMWH) and the duration of such treatment, often in consultation with hospital. The management plan will inevitably refer to recent authoritative guidelines.

6. In view of the risk of recurrence, consider prophylactic measures (e.g. GECS,) where appropriate (degree of risk, immobility, pre-surgery, etc.).

References and Bibliography

General

Anderson, F.A. & Spencer, F.A. (2003). Risk factors for venous thrombo-embolism. *Circulation* **107**: 1–9, 1–16.

Fister, K. (2006). Treat DVT out of hospital with subcutaneous heparin. *British Medical Journal* **333**: 543.

Blann, A.D. & Lip, G.Y.H. (2006). Venous thromboembolism. *British Medical Journal* **332**: 215–9.

Blann, A.D. (2007). *Routine Blood Results Explained*, 2nd Edition. Keswick: M&K Update.

Buller, H.R., Sohne, M. & Middeldorp, S. (2005). Treatment of VTE. *Journal of Thrombosis and Haemostasis*. **3**: 1554–60.

Golderhaber, S.Z. & Turpie, A.G.G. (2005). Prevention of VTE among hospitalized medical patients. *Circulation*. **111**: e1–e3.

Heit, J.A., (2005). VTE: disease burden, outcomes and risk factors. *Journal of Thrombosis and Haemostasis* **3**: 1611–7.

Ost, D., Tepper, J., Mihara, H., Lander, O., Heinzer, R. & Fein, A. (2005). Duration of anti-coagulation following VTE. *Journal of the American Medical Association*. **294**: 706–15.

Turpie, A.G., Chin, B.S. & Lip, G. Y. (2002). ABC of antithrombotic therapy: VTE: pathophysiology, clinical features and prevention. *British Medical Journal*. **325**: 887–90.

Cancer

Lee, A.Y. & Levine, M.N. (2004). Venous thromboembolism and cancer. *Circulation*. **107**: 117–121

Lee, A.Y.Y. (2004). Management of thrombosis in cancer. *British Journal of Haematology* **128**: 291–302.

Lip, G.Y., Chin, B.S. & Blann, A.D. (2002). Cancer and the prothrombotic state. *The Lancet Oncology* **3**: 27–34.

Lin, J., Wakefield, T.W. & Henke, P.K. (2006). Risk factors associated with VTEs in patients with malignancy. *Blood Coagulation & Fibrinolysis* **17**: 265–70.

Nierodzik, M. & Karpatkin, S. (2005). Hypercoagulability preceding cancer. *Journal of Thrombosis and Haemostasis*. **3**: 577–80.

Diagnosis

Fancher, T.L., White, R.H. & Kravitz, R.L. (2002). Combined use of rapid D-dimer and estimation of clinical probability in the diagnosis of DVT: systematic review. *British Medical Journal* **329**:821 doi:10.1136/ bmj.38226.719803.EB

Kearon, C., Ginsberg, J.S., Douketis, J. Turpie, A.G., Bates, S.M., Lee, A.Y., Crowther, M.A., Weitz, J.I., Brill-Edwards, P., Anderson, D.R., Kovacs, M.J., Linkins, L., Julian, J.A., Bonilla, L.R. & Gent, M. (2006). An evaluation of D-dimer in the diagnosis of pulmonary embolism: a randomised trial. *Annals of Internal Medicine* **144**: 812–21.

Tovey, C. & Wyatt, S. (2003). Diagnosis, investigation, and management of DVT. *British Medical Journal* **326**: 1180–4.

Wells, P.S., Anderson D.R., Rodger, M., Forgie, M., Kearon, C., Dreyer, J., Kovacs, G., Mitchell, M., Lewandowski, B., Kovacs, M.J. (1997). Evaluation of D-dimer in the diagnosis of suspeted deep vein thrombosis. *New England Journal of Medicine* **349**: 227–35.

Guidelines

Baglin, T.P., Keeling, D.M. & Watson, H.G. (2005). Guidelines on oral anticoagulation (warfarin). *British Journal of Haematology* **132**: 277–85.

Baglin, T.P., Barrwcliffe, T.W., Cohen, A. & Greaves, M. (2006). Guidelines on the use and monitoring of heparin. *British Journal of Haematology* **133**: 19–34.

Baglin, T.P., Cousins, D., Keeling, D.M., Perry, D.J. & Watson, H.G.. Safety indicators for inpatient and outpatient oral anticoagulant care. *British Journal of Haematology* **136**: 26–29.

British Thoracic Society Standards of Care Committee (2003). PE guideline. *Thorax* **58**: 470–83.

Haemostasis Task force for the British Committee for Standards in Haematology (1998). Guidelines on oral anticoagulation (3rd Edition). *British Journal of Haematology* **101**: 374–87.

Hirsch, J., Guyatt, G., Albers, G., & Schunemann, J.H. (2004). Seventh ACCP Conference on anti-thrombotic and thromboembolic therapy. *Chest* **126** (3 Suppl.)... 172S–696S

Pregnancy

Bates, S.M., Greer, I.A., Hirsh, J. & Ginsberg, J.S. (2004). Use of antithrombotic agents during pregnancy. *Chest* **126** (Suppl. 3): 627S–44S.

Ginsberg, J.S., Greer, I. & Hirsh, J. (2001). The use of antithrombotic agents during pregnancy. *Chest* **119**: (Suppl. 1): 122S–131S.

Kher, A., Bauersachs, R., Nielsen, J.D. (2007). The management of thrombosis in pregnancy. *Thrombosis and Haemastosis* **97**: 505–513.

Royal College of Obstetrics and Gynaecology (2001). *Guideline 28. Thromboembolic disease in pregnancy and the puerperium: Acute Management.* London: RCOG.

References

Aguilar, C., Martinez, A., Martinez, A., Del Rio, C., Vazquez, M. & Rodriguez, F.J. (2002). Diagnostic value of D-dimer in patients with a moderate pretest probability of DVT. *British Journal of Haematology* **118**: 275–7.

Anderson, F.A. & Wheeler, H.B. (1992). Physician practices in the management of VTE. *Journal of Vascular Surgery* **16**: 707–14

Blann, A.D. & Bareford, D. (2001). Factors influencing the frequency of attendance at a warfarin dosing clinic. *Clinical and Laboratory Haematology* **23**: 205–7.

Blann, A., Hewitt, J., Siddiqui, F. & Bareford, D. (1999). Racial background is a determinant of average warfarin dose required to maintain the INR between 2.0 and 3.0. *British Journal of Haematology* **107**: 207–9.

British Committee for Standards in Haematology (2006). Guidelines on use of vena cava filters. *British Journal of Haematology* **134**: 590–5.

British National Formulary (September 2008). London: BMJ Publishing Group Ltd and Royal Pharmaceutical Society of Great Britain.
Available at www.bnf.org accessed 28.09.08
Available at www.bcshguidelines.com accessed 28.09.08

Chunilal, S.D. & Ginsberg, J.S. (2000). Strategies for the diagnosis of DVT and PE. *Thrombosis Research* **97**: V33–V48.

Department of Health (2007). Report of the Independent Expert Working Group on the prevention of venous thromboembolism in hospitalised patients.
Available at www.dh.gov.uk/en/publications and statistics/publications/publicationspoli-cyandguidance/DH_073944
Accessed 02.10.08

Ho, W.H., Hankey, G.J., Lee, C.H. & Eikelboom, J.W. (2005). VTE: Diagnosis and management of DVT. *Medical Journal of Australia* **182**: 476–81.

House of Commons Health Committee (2005). *The Prevention of Thromboembolism in Hospitalised Patients.* The Stationery Office Limited, London.
Available at www.parliament.uk/parliamentary_committees/health_committee.cfm
Accessed 28.09.08

Lee, C.H., Hankey, G.J., Ho, W.H. & Eikelboom, J.W. (2005). Diagnosis and management of PE. *Medical Journal of Australia* **182**: 569–74.

National Institute for Health and Clinical Excellence. (April 2007). NICE Clinical Guideline 46. Venous Thromboembolism: reducing the risk of venous thromboembolism (deep vein thrombosis and pulmonary embolism) in inpatients undergoing surgery. Available at www.nice.org.uk accessed 28.09.08

National Institute for Health and Clinical Excellence. (June 2007). Alteplase for the treatment of acute ischaemic stroke: Guidance TA122. Available at www.nice.org.uk/TA122 accessed 28.09.08

National Patient Safety Agency (NPSA) alert 18. Available at http://www.npsa.nhs.uk/nrls/alerts-and-directives/alerts/anticoagulant/ accessed 28.09.08

Sandler, D.A. & Martin, J.F. (1989). Autopsy proven pulmonary embolism in hospital patients: are we detecting enough deep vein thrombosis? *Journal of the Royal Society of Medicine* **82**: 203–5.

Sørenson, H.T., Mellemkjaer, L., Olsen, J.H. & Baron, J.A. (2000). Prognosis of cancers associated with venous thromboembolism. *New England Journal of Medicine* **343**: 1846–50.

Stein, P.D. & Henry, J.W. (1997). Clinical characteristics of patients with acute pulmonary embolism stratified according to their presenting syndromes. *Chest* **112**: 974–9.

Stein, P.D., Terrin, M.L., Hales, C.A., Palevsky, H.I., Saltzman, H.A., Thompson, B.T. & Weg, J.G. (1991). Clinical, laboratory, roentgenographic, and ECG findings in patients with acute PE and no pre-existing cardiac or pulmonary disease. *Chest* **100**: 598–603.

Wells, P.S., Anderson, D.R., Bormanis, J., Guy, F., Mitchell, M., Gray, L., Clement, C., Robinson, K.S. & Lewandowski, B. (1997). Value of assessment of pretest probability of DVT in clinical management. *Lancet* **350**: 1795–9.

Wells, P.S., Anderson, D.R., Rodger, M., Stiell, I., Dreyer, J.F., Barnes, D., Forgie, M., Kovacs, G., Ward, J. & Kovacs, M.J. (2001). Excluding PE at the bedside without diagnostic imaging. *Annals of Internal Medicine* **135**: 98–107.

White, R.H., (2003). The epidemiology of VTE. *Circulation* **107**: I-4, I-8.

Answers to consolidation questions and case studies

Consolidation answers

Chapter 1
1.1 What are the two major constituents of a clot?
- *Fibrin and platelets.*

1.2 What are the two major coagulation factors in the blood?
- *Fibrinogen and prothrombin.*

1.3 What is the name for the process of clot destruction?
- *Fibrinolysis.*

1.4 What product of clot destruction can be measured in the plasma?
- *D-dimers.*

Chapter 2
2.1 Describe some surgical procedures that carry a strong risk of DVT or PE.
- *Orthopaedic – i.e. hip and knee replacement.*

2.2 Which risk factors are relevant only to women?
- *During and post-pregnancy, use of the oral contraceptive pill or hormone replacement therapy.*

2.3 Why do some risk factors seem to promote thrombosis?
- *By increasing levels of fibrinogen and making platelets more likely to participate in coagulation.*

2.4 What genetic condition is the most common cause of thrombophilia?
- *Factor V Leiden – in its heterozygous form is present in 5% of those of white European descent.*

Chapter 3

3.1 What are the most common clinical signs and symptoms of DVT?
- *Pain, erythema, tenderness and swelling of the affected limb. Findings on examination include a palpable cord (reflecting a thrombosed vein), warmth, oedema or superficial venous dilatation.*

3.2 What other aids are there to help diagnosis?
- *Venography, ultrasound, D-dimers.*

3.3 What are the most common signs and symptoms of PE?
- *Dyspnoea, pleuritic pain, cough, tachypnoea, crepitations, tachycardia.*

3.4 What other aids are there to help a diagnosis?

- *D-dimers, VQ scanning.*

Chapter 4

4.1 How does warfarin work?

- *Warfarin is effectively a liver-focussed poison that impedes the synthesis of proteins dependent on vitamin K.*

4.2 How do we monitor the effect of warfarin on the blood?

- *We use the International Normalised Ratio, effectively the ratio of the prothrombin time on warfarin compared to the prothrombin time not on warfarin.*

4.3 Can you name any disadvantages of heparin?

- *Thrombocytopenia, osteoporosis, alopecia.*

4.4 What non-drug treatments are available?

- *Graduated elastic compression stockings, mobility, hydration.*

Chapter 5

5.1 Which single document provides details about all anticoagulants?

- *The British National Formulary.*

5.2 What Trust body within your particular workplace should be consulted about best practice?

- *The Thrombosis Committee.*

5.3 What is the basis of the risk factor method for providing treatment?

- *The presumption that different risk factors are more likely to provoke a VTE than others.*

5.4 Are there patients who should not be given LMWH?

- *Yes, cautions and contraindications (Table 5.3) include severe hepatic or renal impairment, major trauma or surgery to the brain, eye or spinal cord, known uncorrected bleeding disorders, thrombocytopenia and allergy.*

Chapter 6

6.1 What 'medical' patients may be in need of anti-coagulation?

- *Those with central venous lines, malignancy (greater if on chemotherapy), congestive heart or respiratory failure (including pneumonia), HRT, use of oral contraceptives, paralytic stroke, pregnancy (post partum), previous VTE, thrombophilia, bed rest > 3 days, immobility due to sitting (e.g. prolonged car or air travel, wheelchair), increasing age, obesity, pregnancy (ante partum), and varicose veins (i.e. Table 5.1).*

6.2 Which patient group should be given aspirin?
- *Those for whom warfarin and/or heparins are contraindicated.*

6.3 What is the most common time of day to give the patient their LMWH?
- *6 pm, or thereabouts, purely for the convenience of staff doing the drug round.*

6.4 What is the role of the anaesthetist in providing anticoagulant cover?
- *The surgeon and anaesthetist are likely to consult over the use of LMWH in terms of the use of general or local anaesthesia (e.g. in epidurals).*

Chapter 7

7.1 What government agency has published a major document on the general management of warfarin?
- *The National Patient Safety Agency (NPSA).*

7.2 Why should patients about to undergo surgery be taken off warfarin and what is the alternative anticoagulant?
- *Almost all patients about to undergo more than 30 minutes surgery are likely to be taken off warfarin and given a LMWH.*

7.3 How long should treatment with warfarin last?
- *For as long as the risk factor outweighs the side effects of warfarin – generally 3 months, 6 months or for life.*

7.4 What kinds of patients require rapid induction or slow induction of warfarin
- *This depends on how acute is/are the risk factor(s) for VTE – those with highest risk (e.g. in patients about to undergo orthopaedic surgery) require rapid induction.*

7.5 What is general method for changing a patient's warfarin dose to ensure their INR is in range?
- *Simply to recommend to the patient that they increase/decrease their daily dose (up-titration/down-titration).*

7.6 What is the approximate average daily dose of warfarin taken by low-risk patients?
- *Perhaps 4 or 5 mg on alternate days.*

7.7 What is the approximate average daily dose of warfarin taken by high-risk patients?
- *Maybe 6 mg a day.*

7.8 What patient factors influence the dose of warfarin?
- *Age, use of alcohol, heart and renal disease, weight gain, diarrhoea and vomiting (Table 7.4).*

Chapter 8

8.1 What is the antidote for excess heparin?
- *Protamine sulphate.*

8.2 What are the first actions in cases of excess warfarin?
- *Stop taking warfarin, give vitamin K.*

8.3 What are the treatments for life threatening haemorrhage?
- *Blood transfusion, and possibly FVII and/or fresh frozen plasma as well.*

8.4 Which commonly-prescribed drugs interact with warfarin?
- *Antibiotics, cytotoxic chemotherapy, statins, amiodarone; but see the BNF for a complete list.*

Answers to Case Studies

Case Study 1: The major laboratory abnormality is the high level of D-dimers, which may be caused by numerous factors, such as atherosclerosis and cancer. However, the woman has diabetes, and so this may be the cause. But the key clinical question is whether or not the woman has a DVT, and if so, this may be the reason for the raised D-dimers. Certainly, she is obese, is over 60, and has several clinical indicators of DVT. So, in the absence of the gold standard tool, ultrasonography, the only question is whether or not to give a LMWH. On balance, many would, but would also ensure an ultrasound be performed as soon as possible to help confirm/exclude a DVT.

Case Study 2: This woman's treatment is standard, but worries are the nosebleeds. Investigation of this reveals thrombocytopenia (platelet count < 100) but a normal APTT ratio. Therefore it looks like the problem is heparin induced thrombocytopenia. Treatment of this is to remove the heparin, but this leads to a risk of thrombosis, so that an alternative anticoagulation is required – most probably a drug of the hirudin class. There may also be the use of warfarin.

Case Study 3: This woman is at moderately high risk of an additional VTE because of her history, a present risk (pregnancy), and the presence of FVL. The anti-factor Xa result is at the bottom end of therapeutic range (i.e. as if she actually has a VTE) but is high for a prophylactic dose (i.e. in VTE prevention). The test should be repeated, and if confirmed the dose (20 mg of the LMWH daily) should probably be maintained as she is at more than average risk of a repeat VTE. If she is obese (BMI > 30) then she is at additional risk.

Case Study 4: The patient is at moderately high risk of stroke with several risk factors (hypertension, diabetes, age 71, AF). The first few weeks of 4 mg/5 mg alternate days are developing a history, which, by early November, suggests is insufficient. This calls for the increase to 5 mg daily. This approach seems successful until the INR 3.7, which is too high. However, first the patient should be questioned as to other medication changes (e.g. for diabetes or hypertension). If there is no clear explanation, then the dose should probably be reduced to 5 mg daily but 4 mg Wednesday and Sunday (i.e. average of 4.75 mg over the week). It may also be worthwhile recommending two days on 4 mg a day before starting the new regime, followed by re-testing in ten days to two weeks.

Case Study 5: The elderly woman's target INR is 3.5, so her first three results are acceptable. The fourth (INR 4.1) is only just outside the target range or 3–4, and the dosing officer is rewarded for keeping the dose stable as the INR comes back in range on the 3rd of September. However, the result that follows is unacceptable, and following the previous high level of 4.1, demands a reduction of the dose to 3 mg daily but 4 mg on Wednesday and Sunday (i.e. 3.25 mg daily over the week).

Case Study 6: This profile is very concerning as the INR is all over the place with no clear pattern. There is one dangerously high INR leading to fears of possibly important haemorrhage. The ability of this patient to understand instructions to self-dose must be questioned. The duration of anticoagulation is short, imply a transient risk factor, and so it may be safer to take the patient off warfarin and prescribe 150 mg aspirin daily for the remainder. Yes, aspirin is not as effective as warfarin, but it is probably less dangerous in this case.

Case Study 7: The patient seems to have induced his own surface haemorrhage and would probably be worried he may have additional bleeds, may lose his sight, or even the eye. Nevertheless, note that his INR is entirely normal and this is important as it will provide some reassurance (to both of you). Some may be tempted to reduce his dose of warfarin to reduce the risk of more bleeding, quite possibly what the patient has in mind. However, this will inevitably increase his risk of thrombosis, and if this precipitates a DVT, PE or thrombotic stroke, it could be hard to defend.

Case Study 8: The high INR is clearly actionable according to Table 8.1, i.e. stop warfarin. Consider vitamin K oral 1.0 mg, retest next day. However, with the history of haematuria certainly give vitamin K, and retest daily until the INR approaches 4 or 5, and then resume warfarin. Also consider reducing the dose for a day or two. But the patient must be probed for possible causes. If the loss of blood seems considerable, then take a full blood count and act on the results e.g. consider blood transfusion. It therefore follows, in the case of the latter, that a consultant haematologist will be involved. Don't forget to look for thrombocytopenia (platelet count < 100), and the possibility of drug interactions.

Glossary

Acenocoumarol: A vitamin K antagonist, sometimes used in place of warfarin

Activated partial thromboplastin time (APTT): The time taken for plasma to clot that relies on the presence of various coagulation factors including Factors VIII and X.

Antiphospholipid antibodies: An autoimmune and thrombophilic condition where the patient is at increased risk of VTE

Anti-thrombin: A major inhibitor of the coagulation pathway.

Activated partial thromboplastin time ratio (APTT ratio): The ratio between the APTT whilst the patient is on unfractionated heparin compared to the APTT when not on unfractionated heparin.

Aspirin: The most commonly used antiplatelet drug.

British National Formulary (BNF): The major pharmaceutical textbook giving information and recommendations about all drugs used in the NHS.

Coagulation: The process of clot formation.

Clopidogrel: An antiplatelet drug and so alternative to aspirin.

Dabigatran: A new oral anticoagulant and possible replacement for warfarin and/or heparin in certain circumstances.

D-dimers: the products of a clot digested by plasmin in the process of fibrinolysis.

Deep vein thrombosis: A clot in a vein in the leg.

Embolectomy: Surgical removal of a clot.

Embolus: A clot or fragment of a clot (plural – emboli).

Epidemiology: The study of disease in populations (as opposed to the individual).

Factor V: A coagulation factor important in the initiation of coagulation. It is the object of inhibition by protein C.

Factor V Leiden: A mutant form of Factor V that resists inhibition by protein C and so promotes thrombosis. It is the most common cause of thrombophilia.

Factor VII: A coagulation protein often used to treat haemorrhage.

Factor VIII: The coagulation factor lacking in haemophilia.

Factor X: A coagulation factor that is inhibited by anti-thrombin and LMWH. Activated Factor Xa can be used to assess the impact of LMWH.

Fibrin: A blood protein, derived from fibrinogen, that forms a mesh to trap platelets and so form a clot.

Fibrinogen: A major coagulation protein, synthesised by the liver, that is converted by thrombin into fibrin.

Fibrinolysis: The process of the degradation of a thrombus.

Fondaparinux: A very precisely targeted drug that mimics the action of LMWH but is far more sensitive, specific and reliable.

Graduated elastic compression stockings (GECS): A non-drug therapy that aims to reduce the risk of thrombosis or its recurrence.

Haemophilia: A haemorrhagic disorder the results from a lack of coagulation Factor VIII.

Haemorrhage: Inappropriate bleeding.

Haemostasis: The balance between the forces of coagulation (forming a clot) and the forces inhibiting that process and also removing the clot (fibrinolysis).

Heparin: An anticoagulant that must be given through the skin.

Heparin induced thrombocytopenia: A low platelet count that is caused by heparin.

International Normalised Ratio (INR): The ratio between the time blood or plasma takes to clot whilst the patient is taking warfarin compared to the time taken to clot whilst not on warfarin.

Low molecular weight heparin (LMWH): A safer and more recently developed version of heparin.

National Patient Safety Agency (NPSA): A government body that issues actions and instructions regarding Trust management of anticoagulation.

National Institute for Health and Clinical Excellence (NICE): A government body that issues recommendations regarding the use of drugs, such as in the prevention and treatment of VTE in surgery.

Parenteral: A route of drug delivery through the skin.

Phenidione: A vitamin K antagonist, sometimes used in place of warfarin.

Plasmin: The enzyme that digests fibrin in the process of fibrinolysis.

Platelet: A tiny blood cell that forms a clot (thrombus) when aggregated with fibrin.

Post-thrombotic syndrome: The long-term consequences of DVT, manifesting as venous ulceration, varicose veins, dermatitis etc.

Prophylaxis: Prevention.

Protein C: A major inhibitor of the coagulation pathway.

Protein S: A major inhibitor of the coagulation pathway.

Prothrombin: A major coagulation protein, synthesised by the liver, that gives rise to thrombin.

Prothrombinase: A complex of Factor Xa and other components that together make a 'super-enzyme' that converts prothrombin to thrombin.

Prothrombin time: A laboratory measure of the time plasma takes to form a clot that is dependent on prothrombin but also some other coagulation factors (e.g. Factor V).

Pulmonary embolus: Clot in a vessel of the lung.

Tissue plasminogen activator: The protein that is needed to generate plasmin.

Thrombin: The blood enzyme that converts fibrinogen to fibrin.

Thrombocytopenia: Generally held to be a platelet count less than 100.

Thrombolysis: The process of clot dissolution.

Thrombophilia: A condition where there is an increased tendency to form clots.

Thrombosis committee: A body of Trust staff who take responsibility for all matters regarding prophylaxis and treatment of VTE.

Unfractionated heparin (UFH): 'Old style' heparin, as opposed to the newer LMWH.

Venous thromboembolism: a clot in a vein.

Warfarin: An anticoagulant that may be taken orally.

Index